# The Most Eligible Christian

## Rescuing Our Relationships from a Dating-Obsessed Culture

Brian Kammerzelt

ISBN: 9798642370490

# DEDICATION

To my students.

# CONTENTS

## ACKNOWLEDGMENTS

My deep appreciation to all those who have encouraged me over the years to turn the original online articles into a book. Thank you to every brother and sister who has helped vet, edit, and shape these perspectives in life and in writing. A special thank you to Lindsey Ponder and Mackenzie Conway for using their editing talents to improve this content and prepare it for publication.

# FOREWORD

What began as a series of online articles has grown into this book largely due to the many years of encouragement in letters from hundreds of readers:

> Your insight is so revealing and has greatly impacted my thoughts and will change my actions. I will be sharing this with my young 20-year-old who is beginning to wrestle with many of the struggles mentioned, while friends are starting to marry etc. I know the information will be a blessing to everyone who has the opportunity to read. I was drawn in by each word, each sentence & each paragraph. I found the concepts compelling, critical and an area needing attention by all. ~ Linda

> This comes to me on the cusp of an incredibly tough season of striving and driving for a mate. In the past two months I've been making some tough steps of obedience to begin living for the Kingdom before anything else. Meanwhile, I've not been able to reconcile my longing for a woman in my life, and NO source (fairly well read, in tough accountability relationships, and mentored) has been able to bridge this gap. All until now. This has helped me gaze upon the very face of God concerning my walk with him and a potential spouse. It has provided even more motivation to continue on this kingdom road. And ultimately, it has brought me closer to Jesus. As a youth group leader and mentor myself, this will redefine so much. Thank you so much! Your level of engagement here was bang on, and I think the length was as close to perfect as I've seen. ~ John

I'm thanking you and thanking God for his work through you in sharing this. I am challenged and rebuked by your bibliocentric thoughts on life/dating/marriage and will continue to be as I begin my twenties trying to live a life of service that brings glory and honour to our great God and not just trying to be marriable. ~ Joy

God delivers His wisdom when His people need it, as He has through you brother, and they definitely need it today. I appreciate your long rich thoughts, clearly a great deal of hard-earned life logic that I've just read. Thank you for your vulnerability, and for the faith you have lived by, it is a testament to our Christ. ~ Nathan

# PART 1

# Pursuing Something Greater

Ever since Aimee in the first grade, I had only ever wanted a wife. I never wanted a lot of friends, to be "one of the guys," to be seen as a "ladies' man," or even really to "date." Marriage was my only relational desire. Even at seven years old, I can remember being fully aware of the ideal of Christian marriage. So, for that end, I began to set my mind, steel my character, and discipline my heart so that I might become "the most eligible Christian bachelor" I could be.

I have never wavered—champion of the idealists, the most hopelessly romantic—my resolve has only strengthened. Now, with half of my lifetime passed by and never married, I would like to share some of what I have learned the *hard* way over the years.

## Everyone has lost their minds.

In my pursuit of becoming a "most eligible Christian," I have paid very close attention to the unique subculture that is Christian singleness, dating, and relationship advice my entire life. Certainly, there is no shortage of examples and case studies on the bookshelves and in our churches. The amount of attention we give to "the ending of singleness" has grown astronomically disproportionate. You would think that entire books of the Bible were dedicated to the pursuit of finding a wife, and that Jesus Himself mandated coupling as the chief undertaking of Christian community. Prayer meetings and justice efforts are sparsely attended, but a meeting about relationships is a packed house. Every time.

In this current post-romanticism, Western context, in order to be married, one must first engage in some version of what we lazily lump into the term "dating." We live in a culture obsessed with it, and the dominant Christian subculture has certainly embraced "dating" as their own.

Yet, as far as I can tell, no one has any idea what they are doing. Crazier still, no one can even agree on what they are talking about. **Just ask twenty people what "dating" means or looks like, and you will get twenty**

5

**different answers**: different etiquette, different expectations, different experiences, different everything. It seems each of us is either just making it up as we go along or holding onto personal boundaries or rules that no one else even knows or cares about.

The results are in, and it is unanimous: no matter what conception of dating someone operates under, no one likes it. That dating is "the worst," and no one is having a good time is about the only thing everyone can agree on. For something we seem to be so obsessed with perpetuating, it's all yet another Christian adventure in missing the point.

You can admit, if single, that your singleness can gnaw through even your most content moments with the lure that even those would be better with someone to share them with. How could you not when every song, television show, movie, book, conversation, and even sermon seems to dwell extensively on finding your soul mate? Shouldering the ever-present longing is hard enough without being surrounded by a cultural lunacy intent on keeping the raw nerve exposed.

I have been a part of this frenzied Christian dating culture my entire life. I have watched it consume just about everyone I know. I have felt every bit of the internal and external pressure to be married. I have had every awkward conversation there is about why I am single with well-meaning onlookers. I have never enjoyed it for a moment. This overly heightened awareness that I am alone infects my head and my chest in a way that can ravage my day and take a considerable amount of energy just to keep the madness at bay.

More accurately, everyone is simply lost in a "now for the matters you wrote about" world. First Corinthians 7 is a remarkable passage of Scripture (take a minute and read it closely right now). It's the only passage that begins as an aside as Paul turns to matters that the Corinthians specifically wrote to him about. Then the counsel that

6

follows is uniquely clarified between being his advice as a concession and God's commands. It's as if the Corinthians were saying, "Jesus was the Christ, got it . . . saved by grace through faith, good stuff . . . but Paul, what about getting married?" Paul then acquiesces to their shift in focus. Is it really any different now? Nothing has changed. The amazing revelation of the Gospel is unfolding before us, yet we keep writing in with dating questions.

**This mad mass psychosis over "dating" seems to originate from an utter lack of instruction on a proper theology of relationships.** As with any other area, when Christians are denied biblical instruction, they readily borrow from contemporary culture to fill in the gaps. Yet the popular understanding of dating, sexuality, and relationships is completely incompatible with a proper theology of Christian community. We then do what we do best and write countless books and articles on how to go about a non-Christian activity in the most "christianly" manner—reacting when we should always be leading.

We see a readily observable parallel to this in other Christian media. When so-called "Christian" movies or music are simply knockoffs or spins on popular media, it looks like cheap, inauthentic, cultural pandering. The same thing happens when our posture toward relationship models are also mere knock-offs or spins on what the greater culture is embracing at the time. We end up offering nothing close to the new reality the church is meant to represent.

No answers.

No leadership.

No hope.

The single men and women in our communities are confused, broken, and hurting. All of them. As extended adolescence and unmarried adulthood continue to expand as the norm, more and more men and women experience deeply committed (emotional and sexual) dating relationships while still longing for marriage. This growing demographic of adults has resulted in a lot of questions about self, identity, sex, and relationships few people are equipped to answer. So far, the Christian community has not offered them any relief from their loneliness or bad relationship cycles.

This is a strange era when it comes to dating and marriage, the first to have these concepts totally taken over by a romantic individualistic ideal. One where a man, by himself, must walk out his front door and, by himself, happen across the one woman that is his "soul mate" and, of course, she must do the same in order for them to find an all-consuming love that was divinely designed to create a marriage that rises above all others before or after. **Disconnected from traditional models, and often community of any kind, we find ourselves alone in the search to not die alone.**

Much of the advice I give these days is on dating, relationships, and how to heal from damaging experiences. The cross-section of loneliness, sexuality, family, and marriage has resulted in a pressure point that is wearing on our collective hearts and forcing itself to the tips of everyone's tongues. The best I seem to be able to offer is not answers, but a shoulder-to-shoulder sharing of the burden because I do understand what they are going through and where their communities have failed them.

**The most eligible Christians are the ones who realize there is a cultural lunacy at work and keeps their cool in a mad, mad world.**

## We idolize marriage.

If an idol is something that we construct in order to fulfill our desires while distracting ourselves from God, then I think the way we laud marriage qualifies. Now, we all know that this comes from a good place: the biblical high regard for marriage and relational purity (both spiritual and physical). Christians have been steeped in the ideals of biblical, godly love and self-sacrifice. It should be no surprise that we professing Christians are often the most hopelessly romantic. We are deeply in love with the ideas of love and marriage. No critique here. Good on us.

However, a case could be made that we have unduly exalted marriage and family over the church (by church, I mean the localized body of Christ, not the business of modern church operations). Ask pastors, and they will tell you the order goes: God, biological family, local church. I get it. I've read the books. Yet, I cannot find the Scripture to back this up. Biblically speaking, marriage and family are temporary institutions and *secondary* to the eternal mission of the Church (Matt. 22:30; Mark 10:29–30).

**Nevertheless, marriage seeking has become an all-consuming collective cry from all parts of the community.** We have created a generation of "marriage seekers" who are constantly assured that there is no greater pursuit than that of finding a mate and no greater accomplishment than marriage. Likewise, the chief priority of most single men and women is clearly that of finding a romantic relationship to call their own. An enormous amount of time and heart space has been cleared in order to focus on that end.

We stack more and more upon marriage and have held it up as the prerequisite for maturity, success, stability, and even ministry. Marriage is increasingly seen as the panacea for all our problems—that if we were married, then everything else would just fall into place. It's even advised that certain goals should be put off until after we are married. How can anyone reasonably think or live like this? Have they ever met a married person?

When marriage is your chief motivating force, and not God, you have idolized marriage. This can lead to the majority of our own personal development being tailored toward becoming the most culturally eligible men and women we can be. Our driving force is often not truly conformity to Christ but conformity to our own personal ideal of what a "most eligible Christian" looks like. In turn, the success or failure of attaining that image becomes the filter through which we view ourselves, our self-worth, our success, our "failure" as individuals and as Christ-followers. Like I said before, I have only ever wanted to be married, so if anyone has been tempted to idolize marriage it is me. It is all too easy for your chief personal desire to become your chief priority.

This subtle subversion has forced me to spend a lot of time wrestling with the counterfeit motivation that comes from our own desire for marriage within a Christian subculture. **It is easy to think you are trying to be more Christ-like, when in reality you are merely becoming more culturally "Christian."** That is to say, conforming to the culture's standards of what it means to be desirable and "dateable" is not necessarily the same thing as dying to self and conforming to the image of Christ and His Kingdom. There is an important distinction and a cheap parody to be found here that a *truly* eligible Christian cannot allow to develop within themselves.

**The most eligible Christians are the ones who reveal that what they are pursuing is conformity to the image of Christ—not the cheap parody of conforming to what they think makes them the most eligible Christian to be married.**

## You are not alone.

About here is where people usually protest a bit and exclaim, "But didn't God say, 'It is not good for man to be alone'?" Yes, God did—in Genesis 2:18. God did. We take that verse as a blank check to go about solving our aloneness at all costs. Yet, there is a much more important truth in that verse that should bring such great hope and peace—it's not actually on us to solve! The Creator of the universe recognized this at the dawn of creation—of all things, God, Jehovah Jireh, has got this one!

What's more, that verse is not entirely marriage-centric or even sexual. Adam had no knowledge of such things before Eve. God's pronouncement that man shouldn't be alone was a statement that He created man as a social creature who needed to be in community with an equal and have intimate companionship. We can find that companionship in more ways than just marriage, and for Christians, this is especially true as a local church community. **Within the community of Christ, among the fellowship of believers, no one should feel alone. The degree to which this is true in any given community should be the barometer for whether or not a Christ-like community is being expressed.**

Seriously, take a minute, listen . . .
You. Are. Not. Alone!

Our identity is to be found in Christ and among the body of Christ where we are freed from the relational pressures and expectations of the world. You are not primarily a sexual creature, or a "slave to your sex drive," or even a spouse. You are most certainly not half of a whole—the idea that you will be completed in someone else is a lie and completely opposed to the biblical foundation of dying to self and finding your identity in Christ. Sex is not the answer. Marriage is not the answer. Jesus is the only answer to the longing you feel. We all must detach our *loneliness* from assumptions about *singleness*. Otherwise we commit a caustic error of correlation versus causation.

Just because you feel lonely does not mean the reason is singleness or the solution is a romantic relationship.

Spend any amount of time studying the Bible and you will find so many men, women, prophets, and leaders who went through long seasons of abject loneliness. Consider Noah, Moses, Martha, Hannah, David, John the Baptist, and each of the apostles. All experienced deep seasons of loneliness. Even, and most completely, our Savior. We cannot dismiss or underestimate the significance of the fact (and the dignity to the unmarried it brings) that Yeshua of Nazareth never married and lived unmarried long past the customary age, even though as Christ He became fully human and experienced every desire we do. We can know for sure that God understands, is with us, and is at work in these circumstances. Everyone feels lonely; it is a constant part of our lives due to sin and the separation it causes from God's intended order. You are not alone in this. Single, married, famous, destitute, popular, unknown—all *feel* alone at times. Nothing on this earth will ever fill that void. Knowing this has calmed me down considerably and helped me understand loneliness not as something that we need to "get rid of," but as merely a part of being human. Or in the timeless words of C.S. Lewis, "If I find in myself a desire which no experience in the world can satisfy, the most probable explanation is that I was made for another world."

No, it is not good for man to be alone. (Trust me, this one I understand.) I know exactly why it is not good for man to be alone—and I'm one who has been truly single my entire life, never having a long-term relationship. All in all, I have not been given one solitary moment of contentment in my singleness. I know well the feelings of isolation, of being unloved and unlovable. I know the long dark nights when it feels as if your own soul has turned against you as it screams for release from this mortal coil. The temptations . . . so many temptations—to give in, to give up, to act out, to drown yourself in any of the ungodly releases this world places at your fingertips. The prison of "aloneness." The brick in your chest. The hand at your throat . . . the lies. All lies. Lies from the pit of hell.

Christian community is intended to step in with presence as the body of Christ. We must not leave anyone alone—or worse, perpetuate feelings of rejection and loneliness in others through our careless selfish pursuit of a spouse. I know that it is not good for a man to be alone, but I do not get to define myself by it, let others define me by it, allow it to take over my priorities, or weaken my faith in a sovereign God.

**The most eligible Christians do not let themselves or anyone else define them by their singleness.**

## Many churches have lost respect for singleness.

I don't think I initially respected singleness enough because I thought of myself as "just passing through." I planned to marry young, just like everyone else in my family had done, so being single was to be a very temporary part of my life. I have had to work hard to learn how to be a single adult because the only thing I ever wanted or was taught about was how to get married. I don't know if I have had any true allies in this journey.

**Listen, over half of the US population is unmarried. *That* is the norm, not marriage, and our churches are woefully ill-equipped for it.** What's more, the local church has become one of the most hostile places to be single I have ever experienced. Many of my peers would wholeheartedly agree. Rarely do I see the discipline it takes to be single given the respect it deserves, particularly since being single through your twenties and beyond is many people's worst nightmare. If you have not lived it, you cannot fathom such loneliness and physical discipline.

There are even plenty of ministry jobs you aren't eligible for if you are not married. Why is this? What is the fear? Think about it. Some shallow and simple-minded people consider singleness as evidence of deep character flaws: refusal to grow up, issues with women, sexual confusion, an inevitability of abusing the position for sexual indiscretion, or worse. As if marriage makes any of that less likely.

Like salt to a wound, even if unintentionally, singleness is treated as a gross ailment (contrary to biblical teaching in 1 Cor. 7) that needs to be cured as soon as possible so that a true and full existence can begin—or, at best, as something to come to terms with and submit to. Don't believe me? Then why do we ask people "why" they are single? What reason are we searching for? Why do we look at those who are single through their twenties and assume something must be "wrong"? Yes, we do, admitting that is the first step. Try asking a married person why they are married when the apostle Paul wished it otherwise. According to Paul, we marry because we lack self-control or are content to go against his counsel (Take another look at 1 Cor. 7: 8–9, 25–28, 38).

See, we begin in singleness, and if anything, we are called out of that into marriage. Singleness in service to the cross is the standard, not dating and marriage. Singleness should not have to be learned, coped with, or given into. The idea that it should be shows how committed many modern Christians really are to the dating/marriage cult.

We even go so far as to divide up our communities along lines of relationship status in order to better facilitate coupling, even naming them "singles ministry"—as if that is a person's primary identity. Unmarried adults are treated like members of a youth group by leaders who have no idea what to do with or how to relate to single adults who live in a very real, very physical, and very broken world. These so-called "singles ministries" are often led by a married couple who have no real understanding or interest in what it means to be single.

This thinking builds a frenzied culture of romantic relationship-seeking when we have no idea what we are doing. Unfortunately, the fallout from this cultural mindset fosters the very things it claims to guard single people from: the things supposed to be reserved for marriage are not, the things that aren't are. Our hearts become hardened from being able to experience genuine connection as our bodies are given away, stripping us even further of the depths of intimacy we are meant to experience. We are constantly stealing from the marriage we hope to secure, as more and more shame and baggage are being carried into relationships by people who have no idea how to deal with it.

Moreover, the challenges of being single are simply not given nearly enough credit. I mean no disrespect, but if you have not been single for any significant amount of time, you have no idea what you are talking about. Almost every message I have ever heard or read has been from people who just simply do not get it. It's not their fault—they can't get it. How could they? They've never really experienced true singleness (true singleness being never having experienced a long-term relationship). They have no categories for what it is like when, no matter what level of joy or pain life brings, at the end of the day, you will be alone. Alone to cope. Alone to heal. Alone in the dark. Every day. Their advice falls flat, hollow, and is often condescending.

Now, I am not saying good advice is *never* given or that it *shouldn't* be given by those who lack the experience of singleness, it's just rarely from a place of understanding. As a parallel, I'm well-read and experienced enough to give great advice on marriage communication (and am often asked to), but I don't really understand what it is like to be in a marriage relationship. I can't—there's an internalized connection I do not have the experiences for. Just imagine if a sermon about marriage was given by someone single. Yet messages are given on singleness from pastors who have been married for twenty-plus years and have never even been single (no, your teen years do not count). Often, flippant and insensitive references and jokes treat the twenty-seven-year-old the exact same as the seventeen-year-old.

Let me take a moment to make my feelings on dating jokes from the pulpit clear: **Every time I hear someone make dating jokes, or entice attendance at an**

**event by mentioning all the single people who will be there, I "boo" loudly, and I invite you to join me.** These well-meaning relevancy attempts are one the lowest class appeals from the pulpit you can make and are almost always more damaging than the speaker realizes by assuming, perpetuating, and validating a caustic practice. Please stop. Dating jokes betray the ministry needs of those unmarried and undermine or even prohibit Christian community.

Most advice from church relationship events I have heard is built from two faulty premises: 1. Defining singleness as a "stage," and 2. Assuming dating as a normative priority. At best, it is intended to keep men and women as physically and emotionally "pure" (whatever that means) as possible before marriage. This is fine, yet still entirely marriage-centric and offers little to those of us living in singleness or truly recognizing the realities of this adult life. This well-intended counsel does not dig deep enough into the foundations of our faith nor even bother to ask the question of what kind of relationships we are to be having and what kind of community we are to be building. A proper theology of relationships is typically nowhere to be found. Words that sincerely minister to the desperate hearts in attendance are never offered. Ultimately, these topical dating events are not helpful, and everyone leaves the same as they came. Another opportunity to build up, protect, and actually minister to the unmarried in the community is wasted. We can do better than allowing a dating-obsessed culture set our relational starting point and, instead, proactively create a new biblical baseline.

Scoffing at a single person giving relationship advice (as I often hear) and asking, "Shouldn't we get advice from someone who is married?" only betrays a mindset of something being wrong with singles, insinuating that they are so because they lack the skills to be married. I have been to church seminars based on that assumption. Now, there is plenty of room for some interpersonal coaching and helping people be better with relationships, but let's not confuse the two concepts.

Singleness and celibacy through your prime young adult years take an awful toll, as they twist and bind and wear a soul thin. We are not designed for it. I would not wish it on anyone. What it really takes to be single, to be a most eligible Christian, in this desperate and disparate world, should be seen as awe-inspiring and heroic. Yet, too many modern churches have broken from church history and have chosen to hide or shame those people in our communities rather than celebrate them.

**The most eligible Christians are the ones who hold a rightful respect for singleness and want to help others be God-honoring in all relationships more than they want to make sure they get married.**

## We have lost our way.

The problem is not with the desire for marriage or marriage as an institution, of course, but with the crisis created where the rightful respect Christians have for marriage meets the wholesale endorsement of modern dating culture.

Lacking the proper theology of Christian relationships mentioned earlier, it is through this cultural frenzy, media onslaught, and tacky sermon jokes that the pursuit of a spouse through pop-culture dating schemas becomes the primary interaction model in our communities. In this way, we have let pop culture teach us how to interact with one another: how we see one another, how we think, act, react, and speak to one another have all been taught to us by a culture given over to the patterns of this world. We may combat this strongly in other areas of Christian life and practice, but when it comes to "dating," mainstream Christianity has, for the most part, bought in wholesale to the popular schema. Again, the popular understanding of dating, sexuality, and relationships is completely incompatible with a proper theology of Christian community.

This means we have adopted rules of interpersonal engagement that create a predatory, competitive, divisive, superficial, worldly environment of mistrust. We have needlessly, yet enthusiastically, invited this culture into our youth and adult ministries and thereby reinforced an improperly focused encounter with every man and woman who meet in our churches. Everything becomes about the "romantic qualifier"—meaning that as a guy, every woman I meet is to be evaluated by potentially being "the one" or something else. No sparks? Moving on . . . unless, of course, they have some friends I can run through my romantic qualifier.

We've duplicated a competitive environment where every night after a gathering and the group goes out for a meal, the guy sits across from the girl and seeks to become the most important thing in her life, competing with the guy next to him, and neither looks out for her God-ward relationship first because the one who does is probably not the one who gets the date.

We have forgotten, or chosen to ignore, that everyone is in your life for a reason, and there are far more relationships, deep and meaningful, than the romantic "one." **We are capable of and intended to have so much more than this all-or-nothing mentality that the dating culture creates.** If we insist on our interactions being driven by modern dating practices and romantic qualifiers, we are choosing to needlessly segment the body of Christ and deny one another the familial unconditional love and support that each of us needs and the world was meant to see.

I am as guilty as anyone of letting my own desires and the culture's lens filter how I saw the women I interacted with. To not do so still takes daily discipline. It is fine if I want to meet a woman at church, but it is simply wrong if I let myself see my community as a "dating pool."

I have seen men, good men, walk into an event, and if there was not a woman he was attracted to, walk back out. Even if you don't walk out physically, you may do so emotionally because the same thing happens when you only seek out and talk to the woman you are attracted to while ignoring everyone in between. Or far worse, only talking to her friend so that you can "get to" the woman you desire.

Men, when you look at a woman purely as whether or not she is attractive enough to be your wife/object of affection, then you are objectifying women to a similar degree to other tribal cultures—denying her all she is and the way she is intended to be seen. You're weaving burqas of your own design; immaterial or fabric, the impact on women is cut from the same dark cloth.

Jesus never objectified women, chose His companionship based on their "past," or dismissed anyone He was not personally interested in. In the words of Dorothy Sayers:

> Perhaps it is no wonder that the women were first at the Cradle and last at the Cross. They had never known a man like this Man—there never has been such another. A prophet and teacher who never nagged at them, never flattered or coaxed or patronized; who never made arch jokes about them, . . . who rebuked without querulousness and praised without condescension; who took their questions and arguments seriously. . . . There is no act, no sermon, no parable in the whole Gospel that borrows its pungency from female perversity; nobody could possibly guess from the words and deeds of Jesus that there was anything "funny" about woman's nature.[i]

Time and time again, these objectifying actions break apart church communities. I once watched as an entire healthy adult group completely imploded after one remarkably attractive woman literally walked in off the street and joined the community. The men could not handle the competitiveness for her attention, and the women could not handle the comparison and the abandonment they felt when all eyes turned to her. She was not served well at all and eventually left the community and her faith in a public disaster. Or, look around for the "missing misfit." Has the dating-centered, attraction-hunting tone of your community excluded the awkward and the different? In my church, it has. There is not one single "misfit" who felt welcomed enough to stay.

This "dating culture" may be the most corrosive cultural trend we have ever let into the church—we have got to redefine the way we see and interact with one another as Christian men and women. Of course, that does not mean we need to become a group of platonic eunuchs, but that we have a biblical responsibility to one another as the church. Nor does this necessarily mean leaving "dating" at the door. We can bring all of life and love into the community because we are in this journey together as caretakers. No one has to do it alone.

We cannot allow the world to define our interaction models and then adopt them under the guise of "redeeming" them. Christians are to be about the work of building an entirely new kind of community—Christ's kingdom breaking into this world—a new reality.

**The most eligible Christians are the ones who do not engage in any predatory or competitive behavior, at all, ever.**

### It gets worse.

To say that dating within churches and other types of Christian community looks the same as the world is not entirely accurate. I believe we have made matters even worse by applying a layer of idealism and judgment to the interpersonal alchemy that has got to stop. **Our way is becoming the more hurtful way.**

Let me put it this way: I have sat across from remarkable Christian women and have asked them why they have never been in a Christian relationship, never dated a Christian man. Their answer? "I've never been in a Christian relationship because (and I quote multiple women) what Christian guy would want me after what I've done?"

Heartbreaking.

Convicting.

How did we create a community where that thought is possible? What have we done?

I think I know, and many of you know too. The chief suspects are *idealism* and an underlying sense of *entitlement* that shape how we think about others and about what we "deserve." (A very suspicious word, "deserve.")

An idealism that we have tasted through post-romanticism writing and art and every story we have seen or heard our entire lives has shaped what we are looking for—a true love, a kindred spirit, a soul mate bond. How could we ever go back to any other system of marriage? Why would we want to? Isn't this what God intends for us? Do we not want to experience a deep, unending love that represents to the world through our marriage the way God loves the world, or more specifically, how Christ loves His church?

It's a quick slip from believing that God intends each of us to find our divinely appointed soul mate to thinking we are "entitled to" such a relationship. And from there it's another quick slip for us to think about what we do or do not "deserve" from this relationship that we desire so deeply.

Around here sneaks in the idea that what you deserve is somehow based on your own character or choices (a remarkably unbiblical idea), and with that creeping around our minds, we can often impose our own deserve-filtered versions of our personal idealism onto others. Some even go so far as to carry around a literal list. I doubt God asked Adam for a list before He created Eve. In fact, that guy was knocked out cold for the entire creative process.

Once all of that is coupled with "dating culture" and the average Christian's high regard for marriage, something a bit tragic takes place that is only growing among this generation. As chief of the idealists, I may be as guilty of these thoughts as anyone: **As if *I* can perfect *myself* in such a way that *I* deserve someone *I* deem perfect by *my* own standards. Shameful.** This idealized, judgmental, hyper-romantic, dating-obsessed culture is an antithesis to the radical inclusion and acceptance of the gospel.

Caught in between the true ideal God intends to reveal through marriage and the trouble with some of our personal conceptions and senses of entitlement is the idea of loving as Christ loved. "Husbands, love your wives, just as Christ loved the church" (Eph. 5:25). (Now, if you want to bold, underline, and exclamation point something, you follow it with the words "as Christ loved the church.") Those are some seriously scary words, gentlemen. Complete and total service and self-sacrifice.

Eve was the ideal, the pinnacle of creation, and since day one after the fall, we have been trying to get back into Eden. The angels and flaming swords made a dramatic point then and they should now. There is no going back. Still, every man longs for Eve—a woman made for him, who loves and will only love him, who has never so much as been seen by another man.

However, we do not live in the garden, that is not our world or our reality. We must live between Genesis 3 and Revelation. For us, Gomer is the example. A direct cross-reference to Ephesians 5:25 is the story of Hosea and Gomer (Hosea 1). Christ is the ultimate Hosea, and the Church the ultimate Gomer (various Bible translations characterize her as being a prostitute or simply given over to a worldly lifestyle). This is the image God chose to reveal His deep, unending love that represents to the world through our marriage the way God loves the world, or more specifically how Christ loves His church. We don't often like to talk about this. (Men, don't get it twisted, you are not Hosea. We are all Gomer.)

What does all this mean for Christian community or for "dating"? It means **we have no grounds at the foot of the cross to impose our ideals on someone else and then judge them for it!** Christ did not do so in His community relationships, famously befriending the outcast and the prostitute, beginning His ministry to us all through the woman at the well, a Samaritan whom the Jews despised and who had been rejected by multiple husbands. Even Mary, the mother of Jesus, was an unwed pregnant teen who needed a husband who would accept and love her in a way that transcended his personal desires or standards and cultural expectations.

But we still do it. When you say phrases like "a woman like that," or say to someone else that he or she is not "good enough" for them, we have no idea what we are saying, and we betray our own twisted thinking. Relationships seem to be the only area of Christian life and practice where we are willing to tolerate such egocentric dialogue about what "I" want or about what "I" am looking for—creating this world of idealism and "deal-breakers."

Now, if you are someone who has come from or has given yourself over to the ways of the world—held a lot of different hands, if you will—you can have the tendency to think you are defined by those choices or must expect consequences. Sure, there are consequences, but in the community of Christ, you are freed from those worldly definitions. Your sins are gone, you are a co-heir of the kingdom, fully redeemed and unconditionally accepted. **You are far more than a sum total of your actions, good or bad. How amazing is that!**

We have a tendency (I know I have) to make the mistake of thinking that, if I am holding the line on relational purity that I am doing it for "her," and that if she did not do the same then she could not possibly be the one for me—she somehow betrayed me and broke the contract ("deal-breakers"). I have even heard Christian men say the words "damaged goods" when referring to a woman. That is messed up. I've also heard the retort that if so-called good men and women accept all those who made mistakes, then what incentive does anyone have to stay pure from the temptations of this world? . . . How about God, Christ and His amazing love, the indwelling of the Holy Spirit making you into a living temple of the Most High God—how about *that* for incentive? Is that enough? It should have always been (and should always be) for *God* because that's what He has asked of you, full stop and end of issue. The Christian life just isn't about you, and it is certainly not about cashing in some prefabricated, idealized, judgmental, marriage contract.

I can admit this was a hard truth for me when I was young. Isn't it right to desire only the most Godly woman I can imagine? Sure, it is okay to long for Eve, but we must develop a faithful heart for Gomer too. Hosea was a man of God, a man with a beating heart like any other, with his own desires and personal "standards." Then God said, "that one," and he loved her nevertheless, drawing from a well far beyond his own strength and creating a love story that has been read and reflected on for thousands of years. Romantic indeed.

Seriously, how much "past" is too much to "accept"? Where do you draw the line? Virginity? A certain number of pre-marital partners? Children? Disease? Addiction? Divorce? At what point would you tell me or a friend (or Hosea) that we are not expected to accept all of someone else's choices into our own heart? When am I "off the hook"? It may be a struggle, but the answer must unwaveringly be that there is no line, no limit to the level of love and acceptance a Christ-centered heart must be disciplined to be able to give and receive. The rest can keep their so-called "standards," but we need to be careful with that Christian label.

**God does not owe us anything.** We have got to stop treating our submission to Christ as half of an unspoken deal with God, then getting upset when God does not meet the end we projected. There is no "if I live this way or do things just right, then God will grant me the perfect marriage," or anything else for that matter. It is idolatry. A sexual prosperity gospel. It's the Christian version of Islam's seventy-two virgins waiting in paradise—we just want one perfect bride here and now. It's the same misunderstanding of God. We do not allow for such ends-and-means thinking in other areas of Christian life and practice.

Who understands what it means to love as Christ loves us? The guy who imposes his ideals onto a woman and then judges her for not living up to his standards? The young newlyweds? Or the couples who love beyond the brokenness of this world and show the world the kind of self-giving love that Christ and His amazing kingdom make possible? That is the Jesus I follow, and that is the image I want to at least be capable of representing in this world.

None of us are "good enough" for one another. No two people "deserve" each other. God does not owe us anything, not even our next breath. **Jesus did not die on the cross so you could meet a nice girl who shares your values and settle down.** We are here to learn how to love one another. Not just find one person to love.

For the record, *who* would want *you* . . .? JESUS DOES . . . and all His most eligible followers, that's who! *That* is the gospel to be lived out in all our relationships.

**The most eligible Christians find Eve through redeemed hearts prepared for Gomer.**

## We've ignored something greater.

Rather than leading the way and creating a new and better culture, Christians often misguidedly assume a reactionary posture to cultural trends, then slap "Christian" on things as an adjective and call it a worldview. How we see one another as individuals, as men, as women, is so heavily influenced by the broader culture (and our dating-obsessed sub-culture) that it requires a deep intentionality about developing a proper theology of Christian relationships if there is to be any hope of building an authentic community.

This collision between worldly ideas and Christian ideals can often create a strange and confusing culture of relationships, friendships, and dating in our communities. Is it any wonder why our student ministries and adult groups struggle with a true sense of community and single men and women are the most likely to leave their church? Fortunately, the Bible and Church history have a lot to teach us about how Christians have lived out a vibrant theology of relationships.

Jesus is the living exemplification of His kingdom's relationships. We have a written record of the words and actions that establish our path to follow in our treatment of others. Then, in John 13:34, He commands us to do likewise: "A new commandment I give to you, that you love one another: just as I have loved you, you also are to love one another. By this all people will know that you are my disciples, if you have love for one another" (ESV).

In Mark 3:35, Jesus proclaims, "Whoever does God's will is my brother and sister and mother." Then in Mark 10:29–30), He says, "No one who has left home or brothers or sisters or mother or father or children or fields for me and the gospel will fail to receive a hundred times as much in this present age: homes, brothers, sisters, mothers, children."

What Jesus is defining is the church as the new family of God. Through spiritual rebirth, we each become brother and sister of Jesus Christ through adoption into the family of God. Consequently, we are brothers and sisters to each other. Husbands and wives are, first of all, brothers and sisters in Christ before they are husband and wife. Earthly bonds are secondary to spiritual bonds. Jesus Himself establishes this profound new dynamic of marriage as temporal (Matt. 22:30), but His body of fellowship as eternal (Mark 10:29–30).

Peter directly links to our salvation in Christ with our function as a spiritual family in 1 Peter 1:22 saying, "You were cleansed from your sins when you obeyed the truth, so now you must show sincere love to each other as brothers and sisters. Love each other deeply with all your heart" (NLT). Likewise, the writer of Hebrews urges the church in Hebrews 13:1 to "keep on loving one another as brothers and sisters."

This thread runs throughout the entire New Testament and was taken seriously by the early church. Athenagoras (AD 133–190), in defense of the early church when it was being accused of oedipal and incestuous relationships due to the use of familial language answered, "To whom we apply the names of brothers and sisters, and other designations of relationship, we exercise the greatest care that their bodies should remain undefiled and uncorrupted."[ii]

Athenagoras goes on to reinforce that the early church followed the apostle Paul's counsel in 1 Corinthians 7, saying that, "You would find many among us, both men and women, growing old unmarried, in hope of living in closer communion with God. . . . For we bestow our attention; not on the study of words, but on the exhibition and teaching of actions, that a person should either remain as he was born or be content with one marriage."[iii]

This tells us a couple of things: the early church was carrying on in marriage (hence the accusation of incest), and their primary understanding and care for one another was guided by a brotherhood and sisterhood that looked out for one another as such. Married, unmarried, men, women, young, and old all living in community as a spiritual family. Radical then, radical now.

The church is the new family of God. How we understand one another as men and women affects all of our relationships, and our primary understanding of one another and our primary interaction model from Scripture is that of the brotherhood and sisterhood of all believers—and that changes everything in a world-wrecking, plan-changing, pride-stomping, inverted, topsy-turvy way that Christ and His kingdom do so well.

Now, let's be crystal clear about something: "brotherhood and sisterhood" is not a synonym for "just friends." This cheapens and limits the body of Christ. As the guiding principle of all our interactions, it is so much more. You do not start there and move onto "something more" like dating or marriage. **The something more, the something greater, *is* the brotherhood and sisterhood of all believers! We are given this greater default relationship as a gift of grace, and as with all things Gospel, you do not need to be anything other than who you are at this very moment to receive it! We begin in the eternal. How amazing is that!**

**Shame on us if we reduce the brotherhood and sisterhood of all believers to something so much less, so trivial as some modern dating version of "just friends."** We can do better. We can create a radical, counter-cultural community. Our guiding question at all times must be: "At this moment, am I more concerned with this person's and the people around me's relationship with God than anything else?" More than your desire for a wife, more than your desire for friendship, more than your loneliness, more than your pride or vanity, more than anything?

No matter how strongly I desire a wife, even if my pursuit of that is noble, I cannot allow that to control how I engage in fellowship—meaning, romance becoming my only concern, or positioning, posturing, and manipulating in order to secure that future.

In James 2, Scripture admonishes against showing favoritism. The example given is that of rich and poor, but it is not a stretch to say the same about personal attraction or how we treat one another as men and women. Likewise, in 2 Corinthians 6:11–13, Scripture instructs against withholding affection: "We have spoken freely to you, Corinthians, and opened wide our hearts to you. We are not withholding our affection from you, but you are withholding yours from us. As a fair exchange—I speak as to my children—open wide your hearts also."

We may never withhold our love for someone based on what a "dating" driven interaction model dictates. If you withhold love for someone—as in John 13:35 they will know us by our love for one another kind of love—based on a romantic qualifier, then you have failed the community of God. Fears of someone "getting the wrong idea" are superfluous to our responsibility to one another as brothers and sisters. Being discriminatory in our choices to be open to some people (those we are physically attracted to) and not to others (those we are not physically attracted to) and pushing aside everyone else in our search for "the one" is simply unacceptable.

We settle for so much less than God has for us. The fellowship of the saints, the body of Christ, the brotherhood and sisterhood of all believers *is* the something greater! **In such a lonely and isolated age, there may be no generation or culture in history more in need of the freedom and security that comes from this kind of community than ours. I can promise you, and you may agree, that if there was a community where everyone** could enter in and lay their armor down just for one second, where no one would feel judged, pressured, or compared, where they could truly trust the people around them, that countless men and women would run to be a part of that kind of community. The floors would be stained with the tears cried in relief from the pressures and loneliness faced day in and day out.

The spiritual family of God is now the divine order of things, and God's economy is perfect. We must take it seriously. Obsess over His kingdom, and invest in the body of Christ above all. Trust in Him for the rest. Anything less is telling God we know best, and our needs must be put first or met in the way we insist. If you stop seeking a spouse and start having kingdom relationships, you just might find you'll end up with the best of both. Not that this is simple, nor is it something that can just be told to you. It is something that we must stand for and work through together as a community.

**The most eligible Christians are not the ones hard pressing every new person for a date. They are the ones first and foremost showing a genuine interest that everyone who comes around becomes a part of the community.**

*To love at all is to be vulnerable. Love anything, and your heart will certainly be wrung and possibly be broken. If you want to make sure of keeping it intact, you must give your heart to no one, not even to an animal. Wrap it carefully round with hobbies and little luxuries; avoid all entanglements; lock it up safe in the casket or coffin of your selfishness. But in that casket- safe, dark, motionless, airless—it will change. It will not be broken; it will become unbreakable, impenetrable, irredeemable. ~ C.S. Lewis[iv]*

# PART 2

# Becoming Something Greater

Ever since Katie Wilson in college I have been faced with the need for Christian community, or more specifically, sisterhood (despite my reluctance). I may not have been looking for it, known I wanted it, or even knew what it was, but my categories for women and my understanding of biblical community were about to get completely deconstructed.

After transferring into a new university my junior year, I found myself on the floor of my dorm room begging God for there to be just one Christian peer out there, just one person to make me feel like I wasn't crazy or alone. I got up from that agonized prayer and walked one door down to see who was hanging out with my social neighbors—and there she was. A living embodiment of an answer to prayer. We had yet to meet, and I knew nothing of her, but I heard clearly in my soul (perhaps for the first time): You. Are. Not. Alone.

I wasn't. Katie Wilson was indeed a strong woman of faith and a true sister in Christ to the people in her life. It was through this young woman that I would come face-to-face with how futile my existing conceptions about women really were. I needed more than what I was looking for—an "otherness" to ground me and my faith in this present reality—the "something greater."

As time went on, I don't think I could have messed things up more. One day, while being pressed about my "intentions" from some mutual friends, I went on record saying I didn't think we would have a good dating relationship or were meant to be in one. "So what do you want?" was the logically and skeptically asked question. "What," indeed.

In the two short years at my new university, alongside a cast of remarkable Christians, I learned a lot about how something greater had to exist. The brotherhood and sisterhood had to be something real—and that it was something we were missing.

Katie Wilson became a symbol of this "kingdom reality" to me. As an answered prayer, a needed physical presence, and a faithful representation, she was the Kingdom breaking into my world. Few people have been more important to me.

God saw fit that this lesson about Christian brotherhood and sisterhood was so important for me to learn, but more importantly to never forget, twist, downplay, or dismiss that my actual biological sister's married name became—Katie Wilson. Can't make that stuff up. I am now reminded of God's plan for the brotherhood and sisterhood of all believers every time I think of my sister or hear her name.

## Battle a culture of fear and mistrust.

Without exception, when presented with the ideal of Kingdom relationships and the brotherhood and sisterhood of all believers, the challenge comes: "That's all well and good, but it will never work." Why are we so quick to pragmatically dismiss the Kingdom ideal? The answers I hear always reveal the same thing: a deep-seated fear and mistrust. It seems we can't have the gift of Christian community because we've succumbed to (or perhaps bred) a fearful culture of mistrust. Awesome. I do not think I've ever heard a better reason to reject a dating-obsessed culture and become the something greater in the body of Christ.

As a Christian brother, I am able to look at a woman and tell her the truth: You are a remarkable woman, a daughter of the Most High God, a sister to our Lord and Savior, created and intimately loved by the God of the universe. You are loved. You are seen. You are heard. You are known. You are enough. Do not let anyone tell you differently, least of all yourself.

In contrast, I have been told strongly (mostly by pastors), "No! You can't say things like that to women. It would not be appropriate." I could not disagree more. Why can't I say those things? No one has really given me a clear reason to fear such words. **Fear is most dangerous when it sounds like wisdom.** Of course, the insinuation is they will then think I have "feelings" for them. Or "get the wrong idea." That such words of affirmation cross a boundary and are reserved for someone else. Someone I am not. We should all find that deeply insulting. Ignorant at best and fearful at worst. A posture of fear has no place in the victory of Christ and His Kingdom. Fearfulness toward sin is far, far different from fleeing temptation. Taking sin seriously should lead to strong statements, not weak ones.

If I as a selfish and sinful man find myself compelled to speak life into someone else, then I do not want to subscribe to a code where I am to silence those loving impulses because of a culture of fear and mistrust. Feelings are to be had, and not all feelings are romantic. How ludicrous is it to not speak true things into each other's lives because we don't know how to interact and communicate in a healthy way? Why do we fear affection?

What's more, not only can I say such things, but I do. All the time. Such responses tell me the challenger has never tried it. Which troubles me deeply. A lifetime of results are in, and never at any point has it led to a woman being romantically attracted to me (as if that would be such a bad thing) or ends in them giving me a "DTR" (defining the relationship) talk. If anything negative, it pushed them away due to a lack of trust. Mostly it has helped me play a "big brother" role in our dynamic.

Where does this fear come from? What is it? To be blunt, it is because conservative purity culture traded everything in an attempt to limit premarital sex. We were willing to create such division between men and women and sacrifice the brotherhood and sisterhood of all believers in an obsession to secure that one high value. We learned to refer to one another as "temptations" and "stumbling blocks." We stunted the development of healthy boundaries. How has that gone? As it turns out, a fear of

sex and emotional intimacy resulted in us ending up with
neither greater pre-marital purity, a higher marital success
rate, nor a proper theology of relationships.

The in-breaking of Christ's Kingdom demands our
trust. We are to trust that Christ is setting everything right,
that God's ways are perfect, and that He has invited us to
join Him in that work. Especially in our relationships. At no
point does Scripture instruct us to hide our hearts away so
we only love one other person. We cannot be content to live
stalled in this isolating fear and mistrust. **We must battle
against it. We must love fearlessly.**

For starters, we can stop contorting to some lame,
social-norm mating dances that aren't doing anyone else any
good anyway. This is the opportunity to take charge and
show something unexpectedly greater to people in your life
and to the world looking on.

**The most eligible Christians reject a culture of fear
and mistrust and live as if the world is already as it
will one day be**.

## (Re)learn how to see each other.

Quite simply, for any of this to "work," men and women
have to do the hard work of (re)learning how to view each
other. Especially their brothers and sisters in Christ.
Developing new Kingdom categories takes discipline. A lot
of discipline. Counteracting the immense media onslaught
that teaches us how to objectify takes commitment. A lot of
commitment.

**Superficial and self-fulfilling fantasy views are
learned. They can be unlearned.** These views were taught
to us by the culture we live in. They can be replaced by views
from the new Kingdom we belong to. New eyes to see, new
hearts to love. The lifetime of conditioning that has led to
such twisted views of others and sex is not easily put aside.
Yet, how much instruction and how many counterexamples

are we providing? Or are we just replacing sensational cultural views with a divisive marriage fantasy obsession?

In a dating-driven interaction model, every word and interaction is questioned as to "What does it mean?" in regards to suspected romantic interest. Or, well-meaning questions are asked questions such as, "How do I not mislead?" All such questions assume a romantic dating schema of things as our natural relational starting point. We need to completely uproot and reject that paradigm in order to set a new kingdom baseline. This requires a radical shift in perception that requires cultivating an entirely new mental and emotional foundation. Our default starting point in all navigations of relationships is now that of brotherhood and sisterhood.

Remember, brotherhood and sisterhood is not a synonym for "just friends," so it is important we don't think of it in that way. Christian men and women can never be just friends because we are already something greater. This means you do not have to try to be friends with every Christian you meet. You can't. That would be exhausting. Siblings are not always relationally close, but they are still family. Christian family obligates you to your higher relationships, but it doesn't mean you are going to like everyone, have to be friends with everyone, be emotionally close to everyone, or be forced to spend time with someone who is crossing boundaries. We are freed from this kind of thinking because we have a better relational beginning.

For clarity, apart from any thematic approaches to this content, it should be noted that this isn't just about men's perceptions of women or women's perceptions of men. The kingdom ideal transforms all of our relational dynamics and is just as much about a total realignment of men's treatment of other men and women's treatment of other women as well.

Our task is to proactively build an entirely new framework for relationships that upsets the world's categories and frees us to treat one another with the full measure of their God-given dignity, as well as for us to be able to receive it. We can do better than allowing the culture, Christian or otherwise, to define our relational categories—friends, dating, "the one," and all the rest. We simply cannot allow those shallow definitions to define us, divide us, keep us from important relationships or, far worse, judge and alienate others in our pursuit of romance.

Men: increasingly, the average single adult woman has never had a positive male relationship in her entire life. She doesn't need your courtship. She needs your brotherhood. She needs to actually be seen, perhaps for the first time. Think about all those women who have never had anyone treat them as a loving brother would. Never objectified, judged, or rejected. How much do they need men like that in their life? The value of a good man being present, visible, available, trusted, and safe is hard to overestimate. Don't you want to have that capacity? It takes work to develop that character and no small amount of personal cost.

The broader culture (and our dating-obsessed subculture) has taught us a warped sense of beauty and desire. A twisted fantasy. We must replace that worldly fantasy with something God has declared to be real and eternal. **Not conforming to the patterns of this world (Rom. 12:2) often includes not conforming to so-called "Christian" subculture.**

Relearn what God-given beauty is and submit yourself to learning what it means to see that as captivating. Learn to talk to each other—really talk to the actual person in front of you and freely extend to them their God-given dignity and personhood. Learn life-giving words and tone that do not cross lines or mislead. Learn to see and appreciate physical beauty free of sexual objectification. Relearning how to see women includes counteracting the well-intentioned but ultimately harmful advice that tells men to "see a woman as someone else's wife/sister/daughter." While it is true that we are all connected in a familial way, a woman's identity, worth, or value is rooted in being a complete person created by God. Her personhood is independently and immutably given to her. Not because she is someone *else's* something, and certainly not because she is *your* anything, but because she is *God's* everything.

Still skeptical? Not possible? Well, more than possible, we are expected to: "Do not rebuke an older man harshly, but exhort him as if he were your father. Treat younger men as brothers, older women as mothers, and younger women as sisters, *with absolute purity*" (1 Tim. 5:1–2, emphasis added). "...make every effort to supplement your faith with virtue, and virtue with knowledge, and knowledge with self-control, and self-control with steadfastness, and steadfastness with godliness, and godliness with brotherly affection, and brotherly affection with love" (2 Peter 1:5–7 ESV). Countless God-honoring men and women make the choices required to live this out every day.

**The most eligible Christians commit to the hard work of relearning how to see others and freely extend to them their God-given dignity and personhood.**

## (Re)learn how to fight for women.

Let me speak specifically to the men again for a moment because a lot of this is on us. Jesus was actually quite graphic about this point. In Matthew 5:28–29, He tells his disciples to tear their own eye out and throw it away rather than lust after a woman. Try it, seriously, press hard into your eye socket with the tips of your fingers and start to gouge your eye out. Terrifying, right? Well, we say, "Forget that!" Then we displace the full weight of that horror onto women. We make it their problem. Jesus makes it clear that it is your personal, bodily responsibility. There is nothing to women at all about it being their fault.

**Look, either a woman's virtue is safe with you or it is not**—alone or in public, single or married, in any manner of dress or undress, in any circumstances whatsoever. Are you able to extend the fullness of the brotherhood God intends for her to experience from Christian men? As a man, it is your job to get a grip and reject the lies that you are somehow a slave to an uncontrollable biology. Stop blaming women for your "stumbling." Those are and always have been weak and selfish cop-outs—physically, spiritually, emotionally, and intellectually. It is the Christian version of victim-blaming.

"But men are 'built' a certain way . . ." Let me stop you right there because **nothing seems to turn conservative Christians into evolutionary biologists faster than our perceived limits of a man's character.** Men can absolutely control themselves. We can "help it." Any suggestion otherwise is a lie. The idea that men and women cannot be close or alone or cordial without rending their clothes and impregnating is simply ridiculous. If that is in any way true of you, get it together, brother.

Odds are, you know how to obsess, lust, pursue, pine, and pridefully hang onto a woman. None of those things should be confused with fighting for women. We need to learn what it is to battle back both our own dark hearts and the culture's unceasing degradation of femininity and womanhood. First and foremost, it means being *for* women in the way they need you to with no regard for return.

The most vocal for women's rights should be men. Fight out of solidarity for the countless women around the world suffering untold horrors with no one coming to their aid. Do so because the person who took care of you and will take care of you at your most helpless times of life will most likely be a woman. Fight to pay it back to your mother and pay it forward to those who will nurse you through illness and old age. Fight for her voice. Fight for her dignity. Fight to give her space. Fight to give her trust. Fight to let her go. Fight through prayer. Fight yourself. Fight to be able to give with no thought of return. Fight to be a brother in Christ.

Tragically, with the current stigmas between us, anything polite or caring a man does for a woman is seen as romantic interest or temptation. We are even quickly moving toward a warped world where all touch is seen as sexual touch, all time spent as romantic time, any interest in a person is assumed to be amorous. We allow no room for anything else. That is why a better theology of relationships—one far less divisive and fearful, one of brother and sisterhood—is so vitally important to reclaim.

I get it, trust me. I come from a world of teen pregnancy, particularly the Christian kids. Yes, I have seen scandals rock communities I've been a part of and wreck the families of friends. I've seen false accusations ruin the ministries of good men beyond reproach. I've been told that as a man I can only be "at best, a distraction and, at worst, a temptation." None of that means we can't do so much better. 1 Corinthians 16:13–14: "Be watchful, stand firm in the faith, act like men, be strong. Let all that you do be done in love."

**The most eligible Christians fight for others in the way they need with no regard for return.**

## Learn what to give up.

Give up your relationship idols. Without question, if you have an idol in your life, and are at the same time pursuing God, you need to give it up willingly and immediately. If not, rest assured, God will answer your prayers and come for it. He will shake your tree. It will feel like the hard way because you did not let go when you had the chance. **Sometimes we find ourselves praying for idols**—praying that God would give the relationship/wife we've pinned all our affection and attention on without realizing that we've come to idolize them. How do you think that is going to work out?

Give up your objectification. In *The Screwtape Letters*, C.S. Lewis describes two types of women fixed in every man's mind: the Terrestrial and the Infernal Venus. One is the woman you respect with feelings "readily mixed with charity, readily obedient to marriage, coloured all through with that golden light of reverence and naturalness."[v] The other is the one you are willing to objectify and lust after. One you protect your thoughts of; the other you fantasize about. The one you keep pure in your heart and mind; the other you pursue physically without any intent or commitment. One you treat as your Christian sister. The other you treat with worldly discard. One you see as "pure and maternal" and other as "dirty and undeserving-of-respect." The wife and the hook-up, independent and isolated. What's worse, many indulge in the infernal in some twisted excuse to "protect" the terrestrial, but in reality only protect their own selfish fantasies.

Give up trying to change others through prayer. Pray for miracles to happen in your own chest. Do not pray for God to change another's affections toward you. Pray for others to be blessed and for your heart to have the capacity to show the love of Christ. I've learned to pray this way: "Father, set my heart on who you would have me love, and I will love them." Yes, I mean the plural, "them." Pray for the capacity to love whomever and however many people God gives you in your life. Then commit yourself to do exactly that.

Give up your anger. Brothers and sisters, lay your anger down. Anger is what will drive awfulness in your externalization toward other men and women. I am sorry you are frustrated and hurt and tempted and lonely and unfulfilled. It is not their fault. Lay it down. Let it go. Do not take it out on them. Learn to know when you are doing so. Learn to let it go.

**The most eligible Christians learn to give up the behaviors that erode their capacity to love.**

## Love fearlessly as a family.

Without trying to take anything away from physical marriage and family, it is clear we don't celebrate spiritual reproduction and family nearly the way we were meant to—with a similar unceasing joy as parents who can't help but constantly show everyone pictures of their children at every opportunity. Likewise, **our conversations should center around our spiritual sons, daughters, brothers, and sisters every bit as much as our physical ones**. Angels rejoice when one person follows Jesus (Luke 15:10). How much do we? In the body of Christ the means of our multiplication is spiritual. No one is physically born into the family of God, rather each family member is born of regeneration by the Holy Spirit.

The priority of and call to spiritual reproduction is obviously for every member of the body of Christ independent of relationship status. Centered in this kingdom reality, singles hold not a secondary position but an equal one. Rodney Clapp and Stanley Hauerwas said it well:

> Without children, the Israelite fears the single's name will burn out, sift to ashes and be scattered and forgotten in the winds of time. But Paul has seen the arrival of a new hope. Jesus has risen from the land of death and forgetfulness, and so someday shall all who have died. And Jesus has inaugurated the kingdom, a kingdom most fundamentally known and seen not among brothers and sisters in kin, but among brothers and sisters in Christ. Thus, Hauerwas says of singleness, "There can be no more radical act than this, as it is the clearest institutional expression that one's future is not guaranteed by the family, but by the church. The church, the harbinger of the Kingdom of God is now the source of our primary loyalty."[vi]

I disagree with classifying singleness as an "act," since this truth is so regardless of any monastic choice. **No one and no earthly relationship has any special claim on the priority of the kingdom.** No one has more or less time. The Greek word for brothers and sisters (*adelphoi*) refers to believers, both men and women, as part of God's family and without further qualification or classification; as in Acts 6:3; 11:29; 12:17; 16:1; 16:40; 18:18, 27; 21:7, 17; 28:14, 15.

"It is not good for man to be alone" (Gen. 2:18). "Be fruitful and multiply" (Gen. 1:28). Important to be sure, but beyond the garden, we look forward to the coming kingdom and are to live now as if the world is already as it will one day be. We are not alone, and we are to be spiritually fruitful and spiritually multiply (Matt. 28:18–20, Gal. 5:22).

Can you believe that in your church right now, and certainly in the Christian culture at large, there are unmarried brothers and sisters who have never been told they are loved? Many more who have never heard the words "I love you" by anyone other than their parents. Do you realize that there are brothers and sisters who leave their communities because they spent all their time isolated, feeling overlooked, unseen, unknown, unloved? How can we let that happen in Christian community? I know it is complicated, but shame on us if the answer is a dating-obsessed culture.

Spiritual family allows us to not just deeply verbally embrace others but to physically embrace one another as well in love. Christians should "hug deep." Perhaps the icon of our strange dating culture is the well-parodied "Christian side-hug." **We act like we fear the female body. Let's face it, we do.** We simply do not know how to be affectionate. All those verses about a holy kiss (Rom. 16:16; 1 Thess. 5:26; 1 Cor. 16:20; 2 Cor. 13:12; 1 Peter 5:14)? No way. We say, "Welcome to the unconditional, eternal, family of God! Uh . . . *side-hug*."

A hug is a powerful thing. I have seen a simple deep hug bring both men and women to unexpected tears. So many people, particularly single Christian adults go far too long without familial, physical embrace. We don't like to say such things, but there are things God can't give us. One being human touch. Our humanity withers without it. We lash out in debased ways without healthy touch. In an all-or-nothing culture of touch and sexuality, it may be no wonder so many are rushing into sexual relationships to find basic human connection. Physical touch clearly has a very spiritual component. It connects us. It holds us to the ground. It bonds us to the life and relationships we have been given. We must develop in ourselves the ability to embrace one another both literally and metaphorically—rejecting that culture of fear or one that confuses all touch with sexual advance. Showing the world something greater is possible.

Here again we can draw from the natural example of a healthy family. Siblings and cousins can embrace without any sexuality in the moment or it being weird. Plenty of people have friendships of this nature. Woe to Christians if we impede forming these necessary connections as a result of our dating obsession. Now, as a disclaimer, don't go right out and get carried away with aggressive hugging. We'll just mess all that up too. Many people are rightly very uncomfortable with physical affection. Do not go body bombing their space. Pursuing something greater of kingdom relationships means being willing to start again at the beginning. Baby steps, family.

Spiritual family frees one another to live the lives we have. I still see a lot of single men and women call their singleness a struggle, something they do not trust God with, a handicap, or some temporary misfortune until the unforeseeable future of some new, glorious, corrected starting point. There is a moment where each of us need to stop pining for the life that passed us by. Come to terms with the reality that the life you wanted escaped you.

**Decide to live the life you have been given**. That moment is now. The sooner you make that switch the better. The sooner we help free one another to do that the better.

Single men and women most certainly do not appreciate when others continue to treat them as if they are in some sort of odd teen stasis. However, too many actually have stopped aging internally as they wait for the life they wanted to "catch up." Some simply refuse to grow up or move on at all. Freedom to live includes freedom to grow abundantly and without delay. As Albert Camus wisely noted, "For if there is a sin against life, it consists perhaps not so much in despairing of life as in hoping for another life and in eluding the implacable grandeur of this life."[vii]

Furthermore, spiritual family frees us to make this place home. By far the loneliest part of my week is not the edge of my bed as I end the day, but the moment my hand hits the doorknob. The relief to be home crashes into the reality that no one is home. Obviously, home and family are inextricably linked. A large part of being freed to live the lives we have is the needed help from family to create homes. Sadly, the opposite is most often the experience of unmarried adults. Holidays are not held in their homes. Visits are infrequent. They must always travel to the married families. Their homes are not recognized as such. Their lives are treated as incomplete and unworthy of full attention. Their homes are not filled with family memories, leaving them homesick for homes they will never have. "Always welcome" is far different from "invited" which is still worlds apart from "included." Loving others begins at inclusion.

For many unmarried adults, their spiritual family is literally all they have. Everyone needs to be reminded of and included in the new reality that they now have "a hundred times as much . . . *homes*, brothers, sisters" here and now. A new reality defined by unlimited invitation and inclusion. Of course you are invited, of course you will be included, we're family. It may not always be harmonious, and you can't be close with or friends with everyone, but your place is immutable. No matter who you are or where you are in life, you are always welcomed home (Luke 15:11–32). Thank God for all the men and women, married and unmarried, who are so gifted in helping others create, have, and enjoy physical homes that provide the grounding and rest our sojourn souls require.

All that said, we also need to give the loss of parenthood more grace. The loss (or delay) of family, fatherhood, and motherhood is a heavy burden that we don't respect or talk about nearly enough. A silent death of a part of themselves that single men and women often must simply absorb as the years go by and reality sets in. While we have begun to be more gracious to women on special occasions such as Mother's Day, I have never heard men recognized in this same way while knowing many men who don't just long for children and family, but to be seen and feel the weight lifted.

Growing up, not only did I envision marrying young, I envisioned my children and my family's children all knowing one another and experiencing the kind of rich connections I had with my cousins. A future that has long passed me by. If I ever do marry and have children, my kids won't know their cousins. Now, they will not know my grandparents. At this rate, they might not know my parents. I may never have children.

Do I even want to anymore? From time to time I'm asked if I want kids. When stressed I often quip back, "Do I want kids? I want to be taking my twelve-year-old son camping right now." My way of trying to express how archaic and ignorant of a question that even is. Insult is often heaped onto injury. To feel denied marriage and family only to be treated as if it is all my fault. That something must be wrong with me. As if I need to be reminded that I might die alone by my own devices. Or as if time has stood still and I do not have a family of my own simply because I haven't gotten around to it yet. That I must want to keep going to the same retreats and parties content to live in an endless loop while the life I longed for escapes me.

Visiting relatives on Christmas morning is not comparable to one being woken up by your own children in your own home. Being a great aunt or uncle does not absolve the soul of our natural pull toward creating a family. Not being able to bear children through one tragic circumstance or another is a grief shared by many. Channeling all of that energy toward spiritual family is a wondrously fulfilling part of God's design, but a healthy spiritual community sees and acknowledges the holes that remain. If a greater relational sensitivity is one of the blessings of kingdom relationships, then it is time we give this one its due as well.

As we mature in our faith and Christian practice, we become more human and more interconnected in the way we were created to be—more of a family that will be with one another for eternity. We already know where we are going. We have been left here to help one another see the transformative love of Christ and invite them into these kingdom relationships. Most assuredly, the joys of spiritual life, of living in a vastly deeper and richer reality may be the greatest of earthly blessings. We cannot live only in the spiritual places in-between the physical world. No matter how fallen it may be. The lives we have are here and now. Physical and present. We must free one another to live without fear, with trust, as a family—**if you ever want that war inside your heart to stop, you need to learn to accept the kindness and fellowship of those who care about you**. Romans 12:10: "Love one another with brotherly affection. Outdo one another in showing honor" (ESV).

**The most eligible Christians celebrate, are secure in, and work tirelessly to grow spiritual family.**

48

## None of this is possible without community.

A running theme here is simply that none of this was meant to be done alone. **None of this is possible without the kind of community the body of Christ was meant to represent.** The familial language of biblical community is not meant to be mere metaphorical, spiritualized, or lip-service labels, but are to be actual, concrete, physical types of relationships lived out in this present reality. We must first create communities where such ideals have ground to take root. Otherwise, it is just more talk and moralism.

Perhaps the clearest case for how far many modern American churches have strayed in their view of Christian relationships is simply the fact that all of this only seems complicated or questionable in this dating-obsessed culture. Anyone who has traveled the world and visited local churches knows the experience of being welcomed and treated like family. It is often immediate, natural, and humbling. They make it look easy. Likewise, perhaps the best way to learn to become better brothers and sisters in Christ through our relationships is to go visit, serve, and learn from the global church who still remembers who we are meant to be.

We cannot change by tacking on added guidelines to who we already are. We need a total rebuild—and for that you need the new reality of kingdom relationships to be invited into. We have to create the space that makes change possible. Our churches were meant to be those places (see Acts 2:42–47). Sadly, most church environments I have seen are toxic for men and women to experience, learn, and model such kingdom relationships. We won't duplicate our "good" men and women if our community is not the kind of space that nurtures such discipleship. All of us have a responsibility to actively learn healthy kingdom relationships, or we will never be able to lead the rapidly growing demographic of unmarried adults in our churches.

The ramifications of perpetuating divisive dynamics and not doing the hard work of learning what it takes to model healthy, biblical brotherhood and sisterhood are severe. I fear if you do not develop a proper theological understanding of men and women, whether single or married, you are in for a lifetime of heartache and trouble. Listen, I am from the future, and I have lived most readers' worst nightmare of a loveless life. It was certainly mine. However, there are far, far worse things in this life than being unmarried. That is not the life I am trying to spare you from.

Likewise, I could fill the room with friends and others I have walked with through brutal marriages, divorces, abuse, violence, infidelity, abandonment, disease, untimely death, and so much more. Many of the loneliest people I have ever met are married. Every one of them did everything right going in and would pass any moralism test you could throw at them. They took Christian courtship seriously, seeking family and church counsel. They had the enviable romance and the fairytale wedding. Nevertheless, life comes for us all. They understand what Paul meant in 1 Corinthians 7:28 by directly saying those who marry will face many troubles in this life and that he wants to spare us from that. I could fill your church with people who have these stories . . . in fact, God already has! All of them will tell you the exact same thing: they needed a healthy, biblical, familial community when life imploded. They needed close brothers and sisters they could run to. Many never found it. No marriage can be and bear everything. No one can navigate this life alone. No one is supposed to have to try.

God knows how hard this life is under the weight of sin. To be sure we know He knows, Jesus lived through it. A man of constant sorrows. Even to death on the cross. Jesus had a worse run than any of us—and it's not like He experienced perfect Christian community either. A bunch of fickle, confused, infighting, and literally asleep-when-needed-most disciples on their own adventure in missing the point.

So what then does He do? Mercy upon mercy, grace upon grace, He inaugurates an eternal spiritual family that can transcend all earthly divisions and boundaries (see Gal. 3: 26–29). One of radical inclusion and embrace. Of course part of God's plan would include a way to bear the history beyond the cross. One that applies to all of us at all times no matter what, forever. Our kingdom relationship to one another is the only relationship that can be unequivocally preached because it is the only relationship that does not divide or neglect anyone who hears it. How amazing! Do not throw it away.

**The most eligible Christians are the ones who know the worst relational fate is a life having ignored the greater eternal gift of kingdom brotherhood and sisterhood.**

*God, in Jesus' great work of redemption, was not establishing a series of isolated personal relationships with His individual followers. He was creating a family of sons and daughters—siblings—who are now "all one in Christ Jesus" (v. 28). The saving work of Christ therefore has a corporate, as well as an individual, dimension. For Paul, the church is a family. ~ Joseph Hellerman[viii]*

# PART 3

# Building Something Greater

Ever since Julie in Chicago, my life of adult singleness stepped over a whole new horizon. My world was about to expand as I was brought to places I had never intended to go and people I had never intended to meet.

Through a chain of unplanned life events, and in spite of every personal resistance to organized Christianity, I found myself earning a graduate degree at a seminary in the suburbs of Chicago. This is where I began working more intently on the ideas of Christian community and wrote the first version of this content.

I was desperately trying to find Christian community and live out Kingdom relationships, thinking, where better to do so than a Christian seminary? Disappointingly, it was proving difficult, and the ideas were often resisted. One day, a fellow seminarian came to me excitedly and said, "I found this church downtown, you have to come and check it out, it's amazing." Being graduate theology students, I thought maybe they were modeling healthy community or pioneering more deeply connective modern liturgies. "No, the girls, you have to see the girls!" He was stunned by the beauty and sophistication of the women in the city and the sheer size of an urban community. So, off we went. He was not wrong.

What I found, in addition to a large group of attractive people, is a church that by any academic analysis should not have existed. It was a rag-tag group of mostly twenty-somethings with no building, a small out-of-depth staff in turmoil, and an obvious identity crisis. On one of my first visits, I walked in the doors of the borrowed building to see Julie standing there like a beacon of hope—she was one of the remarkable cast of Christians from college who became a genuine friend and ally. In a time before social media, we had lost touch, and I had not seen or spoken to her in years.

Julie linked my worlds, and I began attending this church as best I could while in grad school outside the city. It did not take long to see what was so compelling about this mob. It wasn't just about attractive people trying to find someone to date, though to be sure, it was that too. They roamed the social scene inviting more and more people to be a part of the growing community of Christians in the city. Organizationally, the church was going through all manner of trials. However, this fellowship within paid little mind to modern church business affairs and went about the work of growing every summer through invitation and inclusion. It was easy to find yourself invited to a restaurant or a home full of other like-minded, unmarried Christian men and women just doing the best they could to navigate life beyond college in the city and to put Jesus at the center of it all.

A few years later, my ministry and teaching career brought me to downtown Chicago, intentionally living just a block away from where this church met. This was an organic community that fought to create the spiritual family they needed. As city dwellers unmoored from the grounding traditionally found with their families, home towns, or even college, they find themselves more alone and isolated than ever imagined. A city can be the loneliest place you'll ever be. The latent pressure and personal desire to get married or be in a relationship never makes things easier.

At the same time, the organized part of the church began to grow and hired staff to try to manage this community. Unfortunately, these were people set against any idea that men and women could be friends or even close outside of marriage and began teaching restriction and moralism. As time went on, the church grew into a modern corporate church, and we all watched as controls divided and dissolved what was possibly the largest and most vibrant gathering of unmarried Christians anywhere. The organization remained, but the organic family collapsed into a shell of "singles ministry."

Within this community, the church across Chicago, and in my new role as a Bible college professor is where much of this content was developed over another fifteen years of unexpected singleness and a commitment to building something greater.

## It begins with the individual.

If your church does not preach, prioritize, and cultivate kingdom relationships, then you need to change things or leave that church. Without it, any teaching about singleness, dating, or marriage will be void of a truly biblical foundation and the community will always struggle to be the spiritual family you were intended to have as an adopted child of God through your relationship to Jesus Christ. Everyone needs to be reminded and included in the new reality that they now have "a hundred times as much" in that present room and all they have to do is receive it.

It begins with every one of us having an individual change of heart about the way we engage others and our communities as a whole. Here are five practical ways you can begin practicing the discipline of kingdom relationships:

1. See everyone. Actually see them, and let them be seen. So many men and women do not get the attention of others on any level. Let the fact that you care make them assume you must be a Christian, because only a Christian would go out of their way to recognize others like that. Be the one that invites and includes others. Never let someone feel like "the ugly one" or "the friend" due to the way he or she is treated so differently from others.

2. Ask for yourself. This golden rule will fix so many of your relationship problems if you are new to this way of thinking. Never ask a single friend about another. Do not ask her if her friend is single. Do not ask him if his friend might be interested in you. Nothing, ever. Doing so is automatically disrespectful to everyone involved. Not to mention fearful and lazy. Want to know something about someone? Have the courage to ask for yourself.

3. Flip your script. Imagine that moment at church, or a retreat, or a conference and a beautiful man or woman sits down next to you. Now imagine some awkward soul on the other side of you. Odds are, come time to meet your neighbor, you are going to turn to talk to that attractive individual. Not that there's anything wrong with the impulse, but there is if you only ever talk to the attractive man or woman and not even see anyone else. Next time, change your patterns as a personal discipline.

4. Check your words. At every opportunity, scour out any objectification and stereotyping. Reject conceptions of others that label them "stumbling blocks," "temptations," or even "unattractive." There is no such thing in God's eyes. There should be none in yours. Words matter. Words shape reality. Such words are unbecoming the new reality of the kingdom.

5. Stop the pornography of all kinds. This includes the emotional pornography of rom-coms, novels, social media, and your own savior complexes. If at any time you've thought what I've been saying doesn't apply to you because you think you're doing alright in your treatment of others, but you look at porn, then you are dead wrong! The men and women in that media count. They matter deeply to God. You need to develop the ability to see others without sexual objectification, and pornography is part of what kills any ability to love in that way.

**The most eligible Christians belong to a community where they are recognized and supported by their individual brothers and sisters as a spiritual family.**

## It depends on the community.

Kingdom relationships must be embraced as a community. It must be a community decision—one driven by leadership—to reject a dating-obsessed culture and actively pursue something greater in the body of Christ. Again, none of this is possible without community. We must learn to begin again at the beginning, as a family.

In short, any teaching on relationships that is not based on and does not turn to one's identity in Christ and our relationship to one another as the family of God is null and void. Here are five ways a community can begin practicing the discipline of kingdom relationships:

1. Start propagating the church as a family. Proactively create a brotherhood and sisterhood among all believers. Preach this message from the pulpit and at every level of ministry. From children all the way through seniors. Every church should have kingdom relationships training for every newcomer and every leader. We must choose it and protect it at all costs.

2. Begin making more women visible leaders in the church. Skip the egalitarian/complementarian polarity, veiled misogyny, and overall nonsense. Women are leaders no matter where you stand on the elder role and whether they are given a title or not. The vast majority of true leaders I have met in the church are women. Much of the ministry work of the church is done by unsung women. See to it that they are seen as the leaders that they are in your church.

3. Change the language of your community. Reclaim the use of inclusive, familial designations of relationship. For starters, stop using labels like "singles" ministry. Especially if you have no ability or intention to actually minister to the needs of those unmarried. Naming a ministry "singles" already dooms it to failure. "Single" is an awful title—as if single means alone. In the body of Christ, no one should be labeled in any way that would make them feel alone. **No one is to be defined by singleness nor marriage—a false dichotomy, ridiculous really, as singleness is not your "stage." Biblically speaking, you are not defined by it all—because you begin in the something greater.**

4. Address the structures of your ministries. Reclaim the integrated, multi-generational, fellowship intrinsic to the nature of the church (Gal. 3:38). This begins by ending the practice of stratifying ministries along relational lines under any labels. Peer groups will no doubt form organically and space should be given to them, but let the structure of your church help communicate the message of unity in the body of Christ and the eternal fellowship of the saints. Let your teaching, curriculum, language, and structure all align to guide your community to their shared identity in Christ and new relationships to one another—especially if they aren't looking for it.

5. Publicly reject a dating-obsessed culture in your community. Stop perpetuating dating obsession from the pulpit. I would go so far as to say, that when it comes to the pulpit, pastors should not speak about any type of relationships other than those of kingdom relationships—those of brother and sisterhood, the spiritual family of God, the church as a family. Anything else can ultimately be harmful to the community. No messages on marriage, not on singleness, not on sexuality, none of it. Why? Well, primarily, because kingdom relationships are what the church is meant to represent, replicate, and disciple people into. Proactively building kingdom relationships within a community is a huge part of what church is to be all about—yet, I do not think I've ever heard a message or seen a class in that regard.

Not only that, but to try anything else is an unwinnable, unenviable, and needlessly divisive position. Many high-quality pastors I know will agree. Just reflect on what it must be like to be up there to give a message on marriage looking into a sea of faces—some married, some unmarried, some LGBTQ, many divorced, most all hurting—how can Christ be extended to them all in that moment? The answer is only through the miracle and majesty of God's plan for the church—unfettered and unconditional spiritual family. Something greater. Anything less will inevitably cause hurt.

Sure, there is absolutely room and a huge need for marriage groups and counseling groups of all kinds—but that is best handled in those smaller community circles. The gathering, and the pulpit, is for the fullness of the gospel and its implications to the new reality and new relationships we now claim.

**The most eligible Christians invest in a community that preaches, prioritizes, and cultivates kingdom relationships at every level of ministry.**

## (Re)guard those unmarried.

Better serving those unmarried starts with day-to-day interactions. To that end, here are few tips on what not to say and how not to define the unmarried men and women in your community:

1. "Why are you single?" Never, ever, ask this question. Single adulthood is a rough road and the reasons why, or the very fact someone is not married, can be deeply painful. To ask that question in ignorance of years, sometimes decades, of life is insensitive at best.

I could be single because I married young and she died. Perhaps she passed in childbirth taking our son with her. Maybe I was married and she simply gave up for no real reason, divorcing me. Maybe she had an affair and a child with another man. I might be stricken with deep emotional trauma from abuse or sexual confusion, unable to be in a relationship. Or perhaps every single woman I have ever asked out has rejected me, and despite anything I try, I find myself alone.

Those examples might sound harsh, but they are all real stories of close friends. I know far too many similar stories. The stories I hear from women can be worse. The point is, you don't know. Unmarried adults live in the very real, very physical, very broken world. Even with the best case "it just hasn't happened yet" story, the reality is most likely a sensitive nerve connected to heartbreak, disappointment, and rejection.

For many, this is not a flippant question. Let's classify this in the same way we do about asking a woman whether she is pregnant. You just don't. Not unless you are in a close enough relationship to be someone they would open up to about deeply personal issues. The reasons someone who wants to be married is not may not be dramatic. Plenty have healthy stories. Just don't risk it as a rule of thumb. This is where God has them. Period. That is that. Nothing more needs to be said. The question does not need to be asked.

2. "I remember what it is like." If you have to use the word "remember" then you don't know. I can't tell you how many times someone has said to me in an attempt to relate, "I remember what it's like to be single." Or, "I remember what it was like to be your age." Oh really, you who married your high school sweetheart? You, who when you were my age, had been waking up next to your wife for the past ten years. You have no idea what a faithful single person goes through every day and the trials they face. Your goodwill is recognized, but your unintentional patronizing is not helpful.

3. "Why not her?" Advising someone you know well and care about to open their eyes to what is in front of them is one thing. However, a least favorite thing is having to describe why a fantastic brother or sister in Christ is not someone you find yourself romantically interested in. Don't make us do it. It's not fair to anyone.

4. "You could have anyone you wanted." Ah . . . no, if there is one thing an unmarried person knows for sure, it's most certainly that they cannot have anyone they want. If that was even remotely true, they would be with that person.

5. "You're just asking out the wrong type of people." Stop right there. Beyond the fact that you probably don't know the person well enough for whatever you plan to say, such statements are very disrespectful to those people (whoever they may be). Review Part 1.

6. Anything with the word "season" in it. Let's just be done treating any part of life as a season that will inevitably be over soon. God does not owe us anything. He may have something far worse in store—and that has to be okay too. Instead of shifting attention to an unknown future, help them see God at work in their present experience.

7. "You have more time to dedicate to God." No, we don't. This is possibly the most annoying myth told most often. Again, singleness is not a special "stage," nor do those unmarried have any additional time for our calling to invest in Christ's kingdom. Obviously, being more dedicated to ministry is one of the reasons Paul says it is better to remain unmarried. However, we can and should thoroughly dismiss the odd classist refrain that singleness should be looked at as a gift or a "special time when you can fully devote yourself to God."

Technically, it is married couples without children who have the most time. (Unless you intend to treat Paul's warnings in 1 Corinthians 7 as some twisted advice.) Dual incomes and built-in support structures create capacity. Do not put that on the unmarried. We all have the exact same amount of time. Twenty-four hours in a day to serve God. Each and every one of us. Our commitment to Christ is to be total, regardless of circumstances. There are no acceptable levels of commitment to Christianity. From day one, being a disciple of Christ has been an all-in, all-or-nothing proposition—a call to completely give up the life we have planned so as to have the life awaiting us.

8. Any advice about rejection (unless of course you've lived through a life's worth). Otherwise, we have our musicians and our poets for that. They understand. Best

leave it to them. A few rejections then marriage is galaxies apart from the amount of rejection an adult single person experiences and puts themselves through. We were not designed to face numerous romantic rejections over the course of an entire life. We live with it every moment. Don't tell us to "shake it off" or "get back out there" or "What's the worst that can happen?" Especially if you don't understand the compound interest we pay.

9. "What's with you two?" Most unhelpful. You are right then in that moment betraying the brotherhood and sisterhood of all believers. Allow the space to enjoy brotherhood and sisterhood, or at least friendships. Help us be free to live the lives we have. Help protect, choose, and fight for biblical community.

10. "You just need to date more." It is not a numbers game. So much unhelpful advice has been perpetrated on this premise. It shows you do not understand singleness or the toll of romantic unfulfillment and rejection. Best stick with biblical advice. Scripture does not talk about dating, only about loving others as a spiritual family.

11. "You are going to die alone, and it's all your fault." I'm sure you think you would never or have never said this to someone. Yet, most advice essentially says this without meaning to. Either the advice is about actions, looks, or points to an internal issue that still puts a brutal weight on that person. One that says either that person is an incompetent, unlovable creep or that they have internal issues making them incapable of love. We are already acutely aware we might die alone, and it is all our fault. We don't need any reminders of that fact.

Sometimes it takes a form like: You just need to _____, then someone will like you. As if it is just mastering the right combination of words and hand gestures that secure a relationship. Meanwhile, that jamoke over there seems to do everything wrong and has a great marriage. You can do everything "right," and it just might not happen. We need no help in obsessing how we need to be different or better, on how we are not good enough, just to be rejected or uninterested regardless.

Over time, due to crushing alienation, the affirmation so desperately needed can no longer be risked. You want to love someone unconditionally, but the world tells you that you are unloved and unlovable. The more you desire to love and be loved, the louder the lie becomes. Letting go of the desire keeps the madness at bay, but how do you hold onto the openness, the ability, and not let the lies cauterize the wound? This is where the "something greater" of the church is meant to step in and create that space.

If you got up in front of my church and asked all those unmarried who thought they would be married by now, nearly every hand would go up. They are all learning what it looks like to honor God in all relationships. At the same time, many are dealing with deep emotional baggage, acute loneliness, and a sometimes debilitating longing for companionship, family, and children. As the years go by, the weight of life grows exponentially and often in proportion to their isolation. A church is not a "meat market" . . . it's a baggage claim.

**The most eligible Christians look for ways to share life and at no time ever define anyone by their relationship status.**

## We know when we cross a line.

You might be wondering how to know if you've crossed a line on brotherhood or sisterhood. We know. The family language in the Bible and church history appeals to our hardwiring. I honestly believe most everyone knows right away when they are crossing lines in their thoughts and actions toward others. Especially if they have even a latent ability to see others as a brother or sister with their full God-given dignity. We are not as easily confused as we let on.

Obviously, inappropriate physical attention is easier to identify. However, it is our words we often underestimate. We say things that misrepresent our feelings, or mislead, or fill our own romantic narratives, or simply hurt others. Once again, the only solution to that is healthy brother and sisterhood. You need people to literally smack you when your eyes start to wander or your words come out wrong. If you are looking for emotional boundaries, I can boil it down to this: Stop feeding your ego with another person's affections. If you are not in a mutual place with that person, then it is not a positive relationship, and you need to start acting and communicating honestly.

In case you need to hear it: Stop abusing each other! Yes, even you "nice Christian guy" types. What would we do to a guy who kept leaving visible physical bruises on a woman? Hopefully give it back to him ten-fold. Then why do we tolerate the emotional damage? If you do not know how you feel, or if you do and it's not a view toward marriage, then stay away from that girl. You are hurting her, doing lasting damage, and messing things up for her. It should anger brothers in Christ to watch a man leave emotional bruises just as much as it would to see physical ones.

**The most eligible Christians take the greatest care that they are acting lovingly with pure, selfless intention.**

## There is value in a code.

Whenever there is a dialogue about what defines a "most eligible Christian" or how to live out healthy brotherhood and sisterhood, it's not long before the idea of chivalry comes up. Like a collective memory, it seems entwined with our culture's concepts of eligibility, romance, and dating.

Likewise, few conversations seem to come up more often or become more quickly energized than one about the character of men and the sorry state of the modern date. The stories I hear from women would be hilarious if they weren't so jaw-droppingly tragic. As much as I haven't thought advice such as this would be novel, it seems some fundamentals are worth revisiting. Where has chivalry gone? Men, what have you been up to that has women so hurt and disenfranchised with our character? There is no passing the blame on this one.

So, for the person reading all of this and thinking, "I still don't know what this means! What am I supposed to do differently tomorrow than I was doing today?" Perhaps the rich tradition of Christian chivalry can create some stepping stones. While not perfect, chivalry does have a lot of biblical merit. Nonetheless, no attempt at a biblical "proof-texting" of these principles is made here because the fact remains that a chivalrous code by any definition, while a good start, still falls far short of the sacrificial lives of love and justice God demands from His people and Jesus' commands to love one another as He has loved us and to love our neighbor as ourselves.

Chivalry is far from dead. Virtuous action lives on in the lives of countless men and women every day. Yet, we have all seen or heard the tales: A man gets scolded when holding the door for a woman. An elderly person steps onto a crowded bus and no one offers a seat. A woman is lazily courted through texting and last-minute hangouts. A fight breaks out and no one intervenes. Injustice wreaks havoc in the world, and men are often nowhere to be found on the front lines. What a world we live in where such basic decency would be longed for. Is it any wonder that the concept of chivalry still lingers with intrigue and triggers a romantic nostalgia?

Many young men I talk to are frustrated because they feel society has not made up its mind on what it looks like to be a man or how to treat a woman. They all would happily abide a code of expectations if someone would just show them what it looks like. You see, that's the thing about virtues, they are not something that can be simply told to others. **To be learned, virtue must be seen, experienced, and appreciated.** Society has a say.

This is what modern chivalry is for—an established, recognized, non-negotiable code of virtuous conduct that represents the standards by which others would know honorable behavior. Such a social contract frees us to give and receive generous action. It makes a statement. It takes a stand.

Now, to be clear, modern chivalry is not necessarily gender-specific. Historically, men have possessed greater physical strength, access to more resources, and positions of power. Chivalry helped balance that. Women still suffer the most indignity as a class, and all men absolutely have an obligation to safeguard women. However, this is not to say women are not or cannot be chivalrous. In my experience, women put men to shame in many chivalrous ways. The first to sacrifice. The first to stand for others. That said (writing as a man), men, I am looking directly at you.

The chivalrous serve selflessly with no thought of return. Chivalry as a distinct code was originally catalyzed by the church and in service of the king to protect the vulnerable. It is no coincidence that this concept is something Christians, as citizens of heaven and resident agents of *the* King, can relate to. A chivalrous man does not say, "I do enough," because it is not about his own glory. Your perceived limits or a low reward have no bearing on the code of virtue you are held to. Any thought of gain or reward betrays chivalry.

If you are not chivalrous to all, you are not chivalrous at all. **Chivalry is a universal fight for the welfare of others shown through immediate and immutable action**. Anything less is not chivalry but a sinister masquerade to be rejected. This means, while romantic and desirable, chivalry is not about dating or romantic pursuit. As a code of conduct, it cannot be enacted nor revoked based on someone's relationship to or rejection of you. For the record, if you are not able to first be chivalrous, you have no business pursuing someone to date in the first place.

The chivalrous stand out, even among other good people. In a small sense, chivalry is in the difference between opening the door for an attractive woman and rushing to hold the door for a complete stranger. In fact, a chivalrous man may not look all that "gentlemanly" or often even "polite." Some of the best men I know are of this sort. The warrior class can be a little gruff at times. A virtuous knight is still a knight. Such a person is often the only one willing to make a bold, chivalrous statement on the worth and dignity of all.

Chivalry is only so in action, anything less borders on cowardice. Morality without action is no virtue. Otherwise, you are complicit by inaction. There is no such thing as a good man who does nothing. Far more than being "nice" or moral, chivalrous behavior is defined by bold, unexpected, and noble actions. The intrinsic action of chivalry creates movement, incites change. To consider chivalry nothing more than piety, manners, or "polite society" undermines virtue as action. Bertrand Russell says it best:

> If throughout your life you abstain from murder, theft, fornication, perjury, blasphemy, and disrespect towards your parents, your Church, and your King, you are conventionally held to deserve moral admiration even if you have never done a single kind, generous or useful action. This very inadequate notion of virtue is an outcome of tabu morality, and has done untold harm.[ix]

Chivalry is strength to be shared, not hoarded nor lorded. Chivalry is about sharing the trials of the day in small and large ways purely because you have been blessed with extra strength to give. In this way, chivalry is a posture of humility, sacrifice, and stewardship. If you end the day having "held back" generous action, you are hoarding what you have been given—an equal abuse of strength to lording power over others.

Chivalry is not a statement of others' inability, and it is a shame anyone would interpret it that way. It is a mad world where decency has been put in conflict with equality. Carry the heavy load anyway. Modern chivalry is a commitment to connectivity, interdependence, and living in community. We need to relearn to receive aid graciously and allow others to practice humility through acts of service. You probably are perfectly capable of taking care of yourself, but I would still like to pay you kindness. It's not that you can't, but that I am looking for ways to serve. To warmly receive a held door or a strong shield is not to declare your own weakness. If the other strong members of society won't receive kindness, it makes the wrong statement and increases the chances those in need will be overlooked or ignored.

Chivalry is standing up in recognition of others. Stand up. Literally and figuratively. Stand when a woman enters the room. Give away your seat to an elderly person. These are public declarations and daily disciplines that help you practice a posture of humility and service. Stand for the rights and dignity of others. As a rule, start with those you want nothing from and can do little for you. Demand everyone be fully seen with the full measure of their God-given dignity.

Chivalry is actively putting yourself between others and harm and offering your shield of protection. Whether the harm is an attacker, themselves, degrading media, negative friends, poverty . . . look for ways to be a safe place. Start by walking street-side when with a woman or child (putting yourself between them and oncoming traffic). A symbolic statement of vigilance. Don't just lend your coat to a shivering friend, personally give it to a homeless neighbor. Intervene at every opportunity.

The chivalrous fight the hardest battles. What we often think of as chivalry (like the above) were peacetime behaviors that tempered the knight's strength when not in battle. However, if the knight never fought wars for what is right, his daily chivalry would lose credibility. Those suffering injustices cry out for a champion and the chivalrous ride out to meet them. **Start with the small difficulties, and you will find yourself facing dragons in no time.**

Men: do not be afraid to join the fray with what might look like an absurd level of concern for manners and respect. In any given room, in any situation, how can you be the first to help? Sure, you may be misinterpreted, but a mad world is a poor excuse for not living as if things are the way they should be. When you give up your seat you might feel odd, but I assure you, every man who did not will be convicted.

Women: much of bringing chivalry back among men is up to you. You are the arbiters of honor among men. Always have been. Hold men to task and call them out for duplicitous behavior. Under no circumstances date anyone who has not first shown himself to be a chivalrous man of character to all women.

Unfortunately, it is difficult to provide specific examples or scenarios of what kingdom relationships look like because we must first identify communities we can look to. Plus, these examples would be different between various cultures given the breadth of social practices across Christianity and the world. It would be imprudent for me in my context to suggest specific behaviors to those in others. The theology is universal, but the praxis may be personal. What's more, the entire concept can be confusing because most of us lack any experience with a paradigm other than what the culture serves up. Of course, none of that is any excuse for not working together to represent a new reality—

that is, the in-breaking of Christ's amazing Kingdom here and now.

**The most eligible Christians publicly express virtuous action to everyone without qualification or delay.**

*You who long for the Knightly Order,*
*It is fitting you should lead a new life;*
*Devoutly keeping watch in prayer,*
*Fleeing from sin, pride and villainy;*
*The Church defending,*
*The Widows and Orphans succouring.*
*Be bold and protect the people,*
*Be loyal and valiant, taking nothing from others.*
*Thus should a Knight rule himself.*
*He should be humble of heart and always work,*
*And follow Deeds of Chivalry;*
*Be loyal in war and travel greatly;*
*He should frequent tourneys and joust for his Lady Love;*
*He must keep honor with all,*
*So that he cannot be held to blame.*
*No cowardice should be found in his doings,*
*Above all, he should uphold the weak,*
*Thus should a Knight rule himself.*
*~ Eustace Deschamps (1340–1406)*

# PART 4

# Now for The Matters You Wrote About

Ever since Kim in high school, I've had more questions than answers. She was it. The first and the ever-mysterious. If anyone started the inevitable dating turmoil we all experience, it was her. Any answers I have found the hard way began when she sent me forever off-axis as young women are apt to do to young men. She wasn't the first date, but she was the first dance that mattered. Our would-be high-school-sweetheart story was derailed before it even began when she chose the DJ over me. It's okay, I was already infatuated with Shannon anyway. Thus began a life of dates and dating with a desire for marriage in tow. Like every young man, I had no idea what I was doing and gave no thought to the idea that there might be an unmarried life waiting in my twenties and beyond.

After half a lifetime being given dating advice, being the advice giver, and being introspective about my own dating decisions, I think I could fix most people's dating lives in about fifteen minutes. That is comparatively easy to the truly hard kingdom work of relationships. Living out the brother and sisterhood of all believers takes serious time and sacrifice to learn to do well. That said, a book about rescuing our relationships from a dating-obsessed culture probably wouldn't be complete without addressing the idea of "dating" directly.

## We're still going to date.

Without exception, whenever I discuss the remarkable gift of kingdom relationships, and no matter how hard I implore people to reject a dating-obsessed culture and point people back to their shared identity in Christ, one of the first questions is invariably, "So what about dating?" I'm always ready for it, but the point feels lost. This incessant bias further reveals our obsession with dating culture. It really is a "now for the matters you wrote about" world. Our questions should be instead focused on "How do we build a biblical community of kingdom relationships?"

Nothing I have been saying has anything to do with dating as a practice or how to go about it. Dating is not what I am taking to task here, but rather the obsession with it. To be honest, I don't care much to assert any rules for dating. Many can walk a righteous line without the need for extra-biblical rules or boundaries. Some people are able to date or court in a God-honoring way on their own, behind closed doors, with the lights at any brightness setting. Others should only date in groups, in public, in broad daylight, with their grandparents on video chat.

Since no one can define what dating is, any advice is personal and wholly separate from the idea of kingdom relationships. Biblical community transcends time and cultures. Applying equally to the tribal woman, the Victorian era man, a culture of arranged marriages, or the lost madness of the 21st century. We have plenty of books on dating and sexuality. What we need to see more and more of are real stories on how to be a God-honoring brother or sister in Christ.

**The most eligible Christians keep dating in its rightful place and at an appropriate level of priority.**

## We don't really want to date "biblically."

The Bible has a lot to say about relationships, about the kind of character one should have, as well as much to say of love and marriage. However, what it has to say about how to go about finding a wife may not be quite what we had in mind:

Jacob had to agree to work fourteen years for the hand of Rachel (Gen. 29:15–30). Moses's shepherding prowess impressed a man with several daughters and was given Zipporah to marry (Ex. 2:16–21). Israelite soldiers were allowed to take an attractive captive home to marry (Deut. 21:11–13). Onan and Boaz had to wait for their brothers to die and then took their widows as wives (Deut., Lev., Ruth). Sampson simply told his parents who he wanted and demanded they go get her for him (Judges 14:1–3). The Benjamites hid out at a party and absconded with some of the women when they came out to dance (Judges 21:19–25). Boaz purchased property and acquired Ruth as part of the deal (Ruth 4:5–10). David killed two hundred Philistines for Saul in order to be given Michal as his wife (1 Sam. 18:27). David killed Bathsheba's husband so that he could take her for his own (2 Sam. 11). Solomon took seven hundred wives and three hundred concubines from everywhere he could find (1 Kings 11:1–3). Esther won a beauty contest in order to become queen to Xerxes (Esther 2:2–4).

Yeah, not quite what any of us are looking for, is it? What's more, in the Old Testament, the Bible can seem a bit indifferent at times on types of marriage—from nuclear family, to polygamy, to arranged and contractual marriages. Then, in the New Testament, it reveals marriage between one man and one woman as the majestic metaphor through which we might glimpse what it means for Christians to be "the bride of Christ." As stunning as it is confounding.

**The most eligible Christians look to the Bible as their rule for life and practice and do not twist Scripture to fit their own pursuits.**

## There's no such thing as Christian dating.

Perhaps by "biblical" we meant something more thematically "Christian." Using "Christian" as an adjective at all should be called into question, and applying it to such an incompatible concept like modern dating exemplifies the point. As it turns out, there is only one piece of advice in the entire New Testament about what to do between singleness and marriage: Do not look for a wife (1 Cor. 7:27). That is it; like it or not, the rest is commentary. Paul literally says that to the unmarried he has no command from God, only his best judgment to be as you are. If the

Scriptures themselves are neutral on the topic and seem to shrug at the idea of dating advice, then who are we to mandate any?

While this is not what many of us want to hear or believe, practically speaking, the "do not look" advice has a lot of modern merit. When left to our own depraved devices, we will not look in the right direction, we will not choose well for ourselves or do well by others in our constant looking. Think about the implications the idea of "do not look" has for things like online dating and social media. Think even more about how much of your conceptions of love and romance come from media rather than from Scripture or biblical community.

How much of this longing and need to fill the void of loneliness was fed by a consumer culture that creates voids, hollowing us out so that we would spend time and money trying to fill it with what someone else is selling? The modern dating culture is a child of the broader consumer culture, and countless studies have been done to show that more choice does not bring more happiness. Staring at an endless aisle full of options does not guarantee you will be happy with your choice (if you are even able to make one at all). In fact, all those alternatives make you more likely to regret your choice as you imagine all of the attractive features you might be missing out on.

For example, more and more men desire to be with the most physically beautiful woman they can attain. Thinking that if they can secure the one they are most physically attracted to then they won't ever have second thoughts or be tempted by some woman in the future—I think we know the folly of that logic. Different is always more attractive. What's more, regret or "fear of missing out" might be everyone's greatest anxiety. This is especially problematic as our culture continues to warp and idealize our definition of physical beauty. **What we are really doing is becoming a consumer of others**.

I see so many men and women caught in this consumer culture onset of an emotionally over-analyzed paralysis of choice—seeming to need a deep, emotional, over-romanticized connection for every decision, so that permanence can be guaranteed and never regretted, leading to more and more idealism and very unhappy people. I suspect the longing many of us feel for a romantic relationship may be intimately related to these mediated cultural pressures as much as they are to our own created design and desires. This is the essence of the "culture" side of "dating culture" that I have clearly become so set against. Adding a "Christian" label to it has clearly changed very little. Perhaps "do not look" really is the Christian response.

If you can rise above the dating obsession and truly change your perceptions, then the act of a date can still be a positive thing (or courtship, which has become little more than a fancy way of saying "Christian dating." It does not matter what you call it, it matters what foundation you build it on).

If by a date you mean "meeting others with the intention of a romantic relationship," and you are able to build upon the foundation of the brotherhood and sisterhood of all believers and not betray that relationship, then like Paul's counsel in 1 Corinthians 7 says, choosing to marry is permissible and also a good thing. However, as a reminder, those who do not marry also do a good thing. So you should feel no pressure from our dating-obsessed culture to "get out there" and date more so that you can get married.

**The most eligible Christians do not derive their cues about beauty and relationships from any media outside of Scripture.**

## There is, and isn't, "the one."

With all of the people in the world, how could you ever know who is "the one for you"? Next time you fly cross country, look out the window and think about all of those towns below. Do not kid yourself, you could probably land almost anywhere, make a life there, meet someone there, fall in love there, get married and raise a family there. How could you possibly know for sure you have found "the one" among billions? Is there a "one" perfect "soul mate" that you were divinely destined to be with? Yes and no. There are probably a lot of people you could choose to marry and be happy with.

However, I do believe there is a "best" that God desires for each of us. God is sovereign and the Bible directs us to have one spouse. A husband or wife becomes "the one" in the marriage bond (not before nor outside of that bond). So, perhaps de facto there is a "one." However, we have turned that basic principle into a fantasy logic. An ideal that only applies to a perfect scenario that exists for very few people. Think, how does that idea sound to someone who becomes a Christian after they were married? Or for someone who has lost their spouse and remarried? Or for someone who is in a challenging marriage? Suddenly the idea of a "one" starts sounding peculiarly anti-Christian.

Only on the kingdom road of Christian life and practice can you ever know for sure because what you can know is what you are called to do as a Christian and where you are called to be—and all down to a remarkably precise degree. There, on the kingdom road, you may or may not find the wife or husband God would have for you. We can allow it to focus our options and thereby increase happiness and assure confidence in where God has you and who God has you with.

Proverbs 18:22: "He who finds a wife finds a good thing and obtains favor from the Lord" (ESV). Within the New Testament context explored above, this proverbial wisdom holds true. Finding a wife is a good thing, and the

Bible has a lot to say to you if you choose to marry. However, like the verse says: a *favor* from the Lord—meaning a gift of grace, or act of kindness and compassion. As with all things God's grace, it is an undeserved gift. We cannot take that verse to mean more than the Bible does. To find a wife or a husband is a *gift*, not a certainty or mandate.

This wisdom can help frame our idea of dating or finding a spouse. You just may not be able to control it all, because the very thing you find may simply be an unmerited act of God. An undeserved favor means that it is not about your techniques or your merits or pop culture's perceived eligibility characteristics that win you a spouse, but about what God has for *you*. I know many would agree it certainly feels like the miraculous, unexplainable gift from God that it is. We should esteem finding a spouse as such.

**The most eligible Christians do not let dating take their eyes off the kingdom road.**

### Someone is getting hurt, that's the deal.

"Dating," no matter what specific boundaries or definitions you put on it, if done right, results in someone getting hurt. Make no mistake, you don't have to engage in dating rituals, but if you do, **someone is getting hurt, that's the deal**. It is simply the cost of putting your heart out there in that way to multiple people. No amount of good intentions or "DTR" conversations are going to help—in fact, it probably just kills the romance and ruins the whole charade to begin with. Nevertheless, value is found even in heartbreaking rejection. We learn a lot about God and this present reality through human relationships, and it is in romantic relationships that we feel rejection the sharpest.

Christ accepted us, loved us, gave us all He had, all He was, and was rejected . . . We, His bride, still reject Him. We deny Christ when we hide our faith from our friends, coworkers, or those we pursue romantic relationships with. We deny Him when we pursue non-Christ-centered relationships and make choices that lead to marriages that do not reflect Christ's love for the world. The rejection you experience through dating can and should bring you closer to Christ.

I know rejection well. Too well. I get this. I am with you on this, trust me. It does not matter who you are or what you look like—this is hard for everyone. Nevertheless, facing rejection is part of being in a dating world.

**The most eligible Christians own the risks and do not let the fear of rejection drive choices in life.**

## Throw away that list.

A Christian psychologist popularized the idea of making a list of must-have traits and waiting until you meet the person who meets that list. Not surprisingly this is the same person who created a "Christian" online dating website, the ultimate expression of list logic and selling the idea of a technologically verified soul mate. **We need a theology of Christian relationships, not a list.**

What is wrong with having a list? Lists go wrong when they become elevated to some divine, unbreakable contract. Or when they anchor the caustic idealism discussed earlier. Have standards—most certainly. Do not abide caustic or abusive people—absolutely. That is not what I mean here. However, if your list becomes a rigid map of your desired destiny, then perhaps the greatest risk is a vicious cycle of "the list, the one, the relationship."

It goes like this: You meet someone who matches the list. Therefore, they must be the one. Once convinced they are "the one" (because the list you made up said so), you become in love with that list-driven concept more than the actual person. Often, as time goes on, you realize this person is not quite the one you thought they were.

However, at this point, you are now in love with having that ultimate relationship and are willing to compromise and rationalize to the point of cultivating a damaging relationship. Once that relationship ends, you adjust the list and begin the cycle again. What can look like or be described as "learning and growing" through experience is more often an exercise in narcissism. The well-intentioned list becomes a tool of rejection, self-isolation, or judgmentalism, and yet another way we become consumers of one another.

**The marriage we should be seeking is the marriage the Bible outlines: the marriage of the body of Christ to our Lord and Savior, the commitment of the individual to their new relationship and responsibilities to the cross.** I honestly believe that if we all began by envisioning a life of singleness in servitude to the cross, then our lives would be better prioritized. By beginning with a view to marriage, we seek that relationship first and foremost and occupy our lives with personal goals rather than the things of God. Commit to Christian life and practice, you can trust that a spectrum of relationships will form along the way, including romance. It is not about rules of engagement, though they help, it is about a true change of heart.

Instead of a list, be open to the unexpected and a call to things you may have never wanted or imagined for yourself. Be wary of developing judgmentalism. Resist trying to control everything with your own techniques or determination to manifest the life you imagined. To start, rather than carrying around a list of traits you are looking for, perhaps these questions will simplify matters:

- Will this person bring me closer to Jesus?
- Is this relationship bringing us closer to Jesus?
- Does this relationship reflect a God-honoring bond (spiritual, emotional, physical)?
- Will marriage unite us as one in faithful service to the cross?

**The most eligible Christians operate under a healthy theology of relationships, not a list.**

## How to go on an actual date.

Of course, many of us will still choose to date. In that case, we must do it well. A date is a unique act of service, a practice in humility, and a statement on the worth of others. The stakes, vulnerability, and need for trust are at an all-time high—a place where a theology of relationships is needed most. What could or should it look like? I welcome the conversation and embrace the trial and error. In the meantime, here is some of the advice I often give young men and women.

A date should matter. Currently, our culture seems to be caught in a paradox of not wanting to make a date that big of a deal ("it's just coffee") yet still wanting a date to mean something special—for someone to make a big deal for them. This strong desire for romance and equally strong fears of commitment or "missing out" clash and confuse, often materializing as very weak behavior. A Christian takes others, their safety, their emotions, and their futures far too seriously to allow for anything less than brave and noble pursuit.

This is more than just semantics of "whatever you call it." Making the word "date" mean something is important to hold onto if you intend to participate under the cultural label. Therefore, a date should matter. Otherwise, we end up with laziness, veiled intentions, all-or-nothing pursuits, hook-up culture, loaded expectations, and all the rest that modern dating is so easily critiqued for. **To put it simply: If you ever have to analyze whether or not it was a date, it wasn't.**

For Christians, the solution is clear. Due to the brotherhood and sisterhood of all believers, just because a Christian man and woman are together does not mean it is a date or their intentions are romantic. In fact, it is vital to this theology of relationships that it is not seen that way. Therefore, a date has to be a clear, intentional act to pursue a re-aligned relationship. This makes a date a big gesture.

However, that is not to say that asking a woman on a date should be that big of a deal. There is an important difference here. The "ask" changes nothing. Meaning, that if you ask and she says "no" your response should be something to the effect of "cool, see you tomorrow." No more drama than that should be put on the asking. She is your immutable sister in Christ (a relationship greater than all others), and you are exercising a non-negatable code of conduct inherent to brotherly love. Does it need to be said that a date is not akin to a marriage proposal or the nexus point of your prayer life or relationship with God? Everyone would do well to calm down and significantly deescalate the pressure and drama surrounding dating, for their own sake and for the sake of all our relationships.

"Getting to know someone" shouldn't be stressful, pre-qualified, or dramatic at all. Doing so is not a date. Everyone should be open to meeting anyone just for the love of meeting new people and hearing their stories. If we don't because we aren't "interested" or don't want them to "get the wrong idea," then we are committing the betrayals of one another expressed above. To help avoid confusion and the ridiculousness that is DTR conversations (by the way, stop that and start living and communicating in such a way where one is never needed), simply use the keyword "date" to make things clear to both people. It is not anything but Christian community until someone says the word "date." As in:

"This is fun, I would like to take you on a proper date." Or, "This is fun, we should make it a date."

A date should be brave. Bravery requires vulnerability. To be brave, a date must matter. Many of the problems with modern dating are a result of being afraid to dive in fully to the experience. A mature Christian is free to do so because of the way kingdom relationships free us to give and receive generous action. We are willing to do so because of the value we place on all others, regardless of return. To not do so is selfish and cowardly.

Sometimes even the best of us do not want to go through all the trouble of a proper date (of going all-in), but brotherhood and sisterhood dictates that we do so anyway. The other person's value isn't under investigation, it is certain. This also keeps you much safer from pursuing someone you are not truly excited about. Are you sure you are even interested in that way or is it that you don't know any other categories? Could you be feeling genuine brother-sisterly love and just not know how to deal with it? Not every person is in your life so you can date or marry them. If the date is to help figure that out, then it only makes sense to do so bravely. Anything less is wasting time.

If you "know" just a few minutes into the date that it "isn't going to work," then you are an idiot. You either jumped the gun in asking or are being unbelievably judgmental. Either way, when on the date, it does not matter. You still give the other person your full attention the entire date because that is the right thing to do. It is simply how you treat another person and how you make sure you are someone capable of giving with no thought of gaining.

We are free to throw caution to the wind. Our identity is in Christ, we are secure in the body of Christ, and we have the opportunity (if not the obligation) to boldly show the depth of our love and vulnerability to others. Christian community and dating among Christians should be awesome. **Christian romance should be a spectacle to behold.** If we professing Christians are truly among the most hopelessly romantic and deeply in love with the ideas of love and marriage, then now is the time to show it.

A man's gestures and treatment of women should put all others to shame. It's high time Christians see to it that they do. What better environment than the modern date to make a kingdom statement that a woman can trust men and be both emotionally and physically safe with them. That their value and dignity are immutable. What better environment to test a man's true character?

A great date is an art-form. Done well, a great date is an art and a mystery. Few things are more intoxicating and memorable than a great date. To try to orchestrate such a thing would be folly. No formula, all chemistry. However, a few guidelines will help you know if you are ever on a proper date. At minimum, a proper date:

- Is inspired: Hopefully, the woman you have asked out has inspired you to plan a very specific date that you think she will love. A date isn't a "hobby" or just "something to do." If you are just going through the motions or have no date ideas, you may not be ready for a relationship. Women, you deserve to be taken on a date planned just for you. Nothing copied nor recycled.
- Is asked by name: Use the word date. Say it bold and clear. Anything less is something less. Women, be open to getting to know a man outside of a date, but reject the "sneak-a-date"—which is the lowest form of pursuit. Those are just a cowardly avoidance of commitment.
- Is asked one at a time: Ask one woman at a time— one phone number at a time. Give her your full attention. Advice about dating multiple people at once is ridiculous. No good can come from trying to cultivate romantic feelings for more than one person at a time. Women, if he is asking out a lot of women, then you can't be that special to him and he is not being chivalrous toward you.
- Is asked well in advance: At least days if not a week. This takes commitment and is far less likely to be a "game." Besides, you are going to need the time to plan. Women, you have no obligation to respond

to last-minute hang out requests and lazy nondescript invitations.

- Is asked in person: Nothing makes a man feel more like one than walking across a room and asking a woman out, and it makes you more attractive too. If you are not ready to do that, then you are not ready for anything that follows anyway. This means a date cannot be asked via text. Letting technology mediate for you weakens both resolve and character. Women, you have no obligation to respond at all to a date asked by text.

- Is a three-part date: All stories have a beginning, middle, and an end. This could be a walk, dinner, and dessert. Anything really. Small or large. The point is that it takes thoughtfulness, planning, timing, and enough variety to really get to know someone. This means "coffee" is not a proper date and never was. Sorry. Women, if he shows up and there is no plan, then the date is void.

- Is prepared for: You may need to scout locations, think or even walk through the timing, meet restaurant hosts, have friends help set up details, or whatever it takes to make sure the date goes as effortlessly as possible. The challenge in putting together a great date is vastly underestimated. Do the work. Women, if he shows up thirty minutes late without good reason you have no obligation to go anywhere with him.

- Is groomed for: Apparently it needs to be said that a man should clean himself up and put himself together for a date. That means dressing appropriately for the plans and for what your date will wear. When in doubt, dress up a bit more than you think your date will. Women, if your date did not get ready for you, then he is not ready for you.

- Is held onto loosely: No matter how much you prepare, things might not go right. Let it go. You are with her and that is all that matters. Don't stress about timing, don't push or get frustrated. It is not worth it and will only detract from the time you have. Have fun no matter what you are (or are not) doing. Women, proper dates are a lot of pressure, see how a man handles it, but give him a lot of grace.

- Is paid for: First date, second date, any official date, the one who asks is who pays. Do not think twice about it. It's not about gender roles or income. It is about putting her first. What it is not about is impressing her with spending. On a proper date, you pay because money is nothing compared to showing a woman what it is to be treated well by a good man. Women, let us pay (we need the practice in sacrifice), and if a man makes any issue of it or is spending to impress, send him away. Do I even need to say that no matter how much you spend (which is your choice by the way) she doesn't owe you anything? Nothing. Not even a thank you. If you ever get that evil sinful impulse of being owed affection of any kind because of your "investment," you kill it. Stab it in the heart and pray for it to be sent to the Pit. Let no part of that dark seed take hold.

- Begins at the door: This door might be metaphorical. Modern chivalry dictates that you meet her wherever she feels safest. This might be a very public coffee shop. She has no obligation to reveal where she lives. Dates begin at this "door." Which means you pick her up in person. Women, do not go to him or get into a car with a man who did not get out to meet you.

- Ends at the door: If you find yourself at the door to her home at the end of the date, you do not go in. Not even innocently. Keep some chivalry and mystery. The date is over. Do not text her on the way home. The date ended at the door. Keep your cool. This will also keep you from rushing in either out of desperation or hormones. Women, do not invite him in. If he tries to come in, he is not a chivalrous man.

- Is followed up the next day: Contact her the next day at very least to thank her for her time. The rest is up to you, but let nothing stop you no matter how the date went. Women, if he does not contact you or tries some other "third-day" game, he is listening to the world and not abiding by an honorable code.

Anything less, and I am not sure what you are up to, but it is not a proper date. Women, remember, you are the arbiters of honor among men. Send the clowns to the back of the line. Sure, let them try again if they show the ability to grow, but please stop accepting such mediocrity.

Now, I am not saying there are not all kinds of other less formal types of intentional time together as dates—from coffee to sightseeing to activities. Just that, for our purposes here, those are not "proper dates." Perhaps you have already spent a lot of time together in Christian community or as friends. Maybe you need some precursor dates to see if there is more in store. The "just coffee" isn't the proper date, but it may be where you get asked out on one. Then allow that clarity to create bold actions.

Men: Ask! I cannot tell you how many women have told me when questioned, "Why him?" have answered, "because he asked." Do not waste a single thought on why she might say no. As far as you are concerned, there is no reason. Don't make one up. It's her job to have reasons why she would reject you. Not yours. Never forget, getting rejected has a zero-sum effect on your attitudes toward her or the next woman.

Women: There is no such thing as a "bad" date with a chivalrous Christian man. Just a nice time (hopefully) being treated well. While such a date should be impressive, for a noble man, it is not even about being impressive. Such a man is not playing games and is most certainly worth giving a chance at romance.

If the date does not lead to the romantic journey you were hoping for, while the disappointment may be real and the emotions felt are deep, prioritizing brother and sisterhood means that returning to that relational starting point should not be dramatic. That's not to say it will be easy or that you'll be able to spend time in the same spaces right away, but that you are in no way defined by it. Terms such as "breakup" or "my ex" are more lame cultural labels of the dating-obsessed culture to reject.

After that, you are either back at the start, or you are into relationship territory now, and it is up to you and your community how to proceed. I will not attempt romantic relationship advice here except to never forget your default greater relationship and that, if you do find yourself in a romantic one as well, do not drop out of the community. Do not act like you got what you really came for and insulate yourselves from others. Doing so not only betrays the body of Christ but will likely be what ends the relationship you have chosen as more precious. Do not lose your mind or get lost. Continue to reject dating obsession. Let the "burning with passion" (1 Cor. 7:9) mean romantic love and fidelity and not just sexual desire. Keep the greater things at the center of your life and all your relationships.

## The most eligible Christians make romance a spectacle to behold.

Which brings us full circle. The only true theology of relationships is that of the brotherhood and sisterhood of all believers. This is what we should be obsessed with, what we as Christians are truly "eligible" for, as in "having the right to do or obtain something; satisfying the appropriate conditions." There is nothing even close to be found in our modern dating obsession and marriage idolization cults. To be most eligible Christians is to receive the eternal gift that is the body of Christ and live into that new reality.

> *If we consider the unblushing promises of reward and the staggering nature of the rewards promised in the Gospels, it would seem that Our Lord finds our desire not too strong, but too weak. We are half-hearted creatures, fooling about with drink and sex and ambition when infinite joy is offered us, like an ignorant children who want to go on making mud pies in a slum because he cannot imagine what is meant by the offer of a holiday at the sea. We are far too easily pleased. ~ CS Lewis*[x]

# CONCLUSION
## Life as a cautionary tale.

It is an odd thing, being a cautionary tale. "My own worst nightmare." "My student's greatest fear." "A fate I would wish on no one." Yet I have an amazing life. One far beyond my own imagination. That is the point. Perhaps that's the definition of being blessed: letting God fill your life with His amazing imaginative purpose. Here I sit as the steward of a life that I can honestly and confidently say I had no real hand in orchestrating. Knowing what I know now, I truly and deeply wish the same for everyone.

So this is the summary of what I have learned the hard way over the years. Still an unwavering hopelessly romantic idealist. Yet what I am fighting for, to become, to champion, has changed. The ideal I pursue and what I think it means to be a most eligible Christian bachelor now looks very different. May God continue to graciously strengthen my resolve. I am going to need it.

Brothers and sisters, I implore you, reject a dating-obsessed culture. Actively pursue something greater. The something more, the something greater, *is* the brotherhood and sisterhood of all believers! We are given this greater default relationship as a gift of grace. And as with all things gospel, you do not need to be anything other than who you are at this very moment to receive it! We begin in the eternal. How amazing is that!

# AFTERWARD

My goal has been to start an important conversation within Christian communities and provide some basic language and fundamental steps that might help us move forward. After reading this book, I know you will likely still have questions (and I would love to hear them). A proper, holistic, biblical, and theological exploration of these concepts in the context of all our relationships is in order as a follow-up text in development, entitled: *Kingdom Relationships*. In the meantime, for further reading I recommend:

- *Life Together: The Classic Exploration of Christian in Community* by Dietrich Bonhoeffer
- *Divine Sex: A compelling Vision for Christian Relationships in a Hypersensualized Age* by Johnathan Grant
- *The Meaning of Marriage: Facing the Complexities of Commitment with the Wisdom of God* by Timothy Keller

<sup>i</sup> Sayers, Dorothy L., *Are Woman Human? Astute and Witty Essays on the Role of Women in Society*, "The Human-Not-Quite-Human" (Grand Rapids, MI: Eerdmans, 2005), 68.

<sup>ii</sup> Athenagoras, *The Sacred Writings of Athenagoras* (Germany: Jazzybee Verlag, 2012), 30.

<sup>iii</sup> Ibid., 30-31.

<sup>iv</sup> Lewis, C.S., *The Four Loves*, (New York: HarperOne, 2017), 155–156.

<sup>v</sup> Lewis, C.S., The Screwtape Letters (New York, HarperOne, 201), 108.

<sup>vi</sup> Clapp, Rodney, Families at the Crossroads: Beyond Traditional & Modern Options, (Downers Grove, IL: InterVarsity Press, 1993), 101.

<sup>vii</sup> Camus, Albert, *The Myth of Sisyphus and Other Essays* (New York: Knopf Doubleday, 2012) 153.

<sup>viii</sup> Hellerman, Joseph H., *When the Church was a Family: Recapturing Jesus' Vision for Authentic Christian Community* (Nasvhille: B&H Academic, 2009), 96.

<sup>ix</sup> Russel, Bertrand, Human Society in Ethics and Politics (London & New York: Routledge Classics, 2010), 27.

<sup>x</sup> Lewis, C.S., The Weight of Glory (New York: HarperOne, 2001 ), 26.

Made in United States
North Haven, CT
08 May 2022

19027871R00059